Because God Said So

Published by Davis Mission 6079 Thorp Hallow, KillBuck, New York 14748

Table of Contents

Preface

Hebrews 1:3

"Who being the brightness of his glory, and the express image of his person, and upholding all things by the **word of his power**."

Psalms 19:14

"Let the **words of my mouth**, and the meditation of my heart, be acceptable in thy sight, O LORD, my strength, and my redeemer."

While reflecting on all of the things that God has said, I couldn't start this book without starting where God started, "In The Beginning." The Bible tells us, in the first chapter of Genesis, that God created the world. I have often pictured, in my mind, this story of the Bible. I have pondered the fact that God didn't have dirt, or clay, or any other substance in His pockets. He didn't start with some atoms or cells or anything. God used only His words to create. The world and everything in it was created...just *Because He Said So*! The sun, the moon, the animals, the trees, the oceans, the mountains and valleys were all created, including Adam and Eve...*Because God Said So*. God spoke at least eleven times in Genesis chapter one alone. And each time that He spoke, He created something out of nothing, just by the power of His words. God's words were so powerful and creative that the earth exploded with life. Trees gave birth to trees, fish filled the seas. All over the world life was created, all by the power of God's voice.

A few years back, I took some time to circle, in my Bible, every place where it was written that, "God spoke." I found hundreds of occasions when God communicated by speaking. If God's spoken word is so powerful, and we are created in the image of God, then wouldn't it be reasonable to conclude that what we say has power too? I believe it is for this reason, we are told in **Proverbs 18:21**, that the power of life and death is in the tongue. We have the power of life when we speak. Our words also have the power of death. We only have this power because we were created in God's image and therefore our words have power too.

Proverbs 18:21

"Death and life are in the power of the tongue: and they that love it shall eat the fruit thereof."

I don't think there is anything more cruel or heartbreaking then cutting words of criticism. The old adage, "sticks and stones may break my bones but words or names will never hurt me" rings hollow at best. Words and mocking names do hurt. Not only do they bring hurt but death as well. Imagine what it would be like if we could be more God-like when we speak. Instead of death we would create happiness, joy, healing, you name it. There is an endless list of things we could do just because "we said so."

Don't misunderstand me. This book is about what God has said and the power behind His words. However, God's words also empower us to be more like Him...*Because He Said So.*

Special Thanks

First I want to thank the Lord Jesus for giving me the gift of hearing His voice. While I have a long ways to go in developing this gift, I am blessed that I have come on this special journey with Him. I give Him all the Glory and I am so thankful!

Second I want to thank my family who have made this journey with me. I especially thank my husband Fred, who has always been my greatest encouragement. I want to thank Mary, Christine, Judith, and my sister Cheri for their input and help.

Chapter 1
Hearing God's Voice

The year was 1980. My son, Christopher, was only a few minutes old when the delivery doctor asked me a question. As I answered him, my newborn baby, nestled in the arms of his father, turned his head towards me and opened his little eyes. He knew my voice. He was familiar with that sound. He knew me, because he had been listening to me for the previous nine months. Babies are born knowing their mother's voice. In the same way, we are all born with the ability to hear God.

Some years ago, my dad was invited to be the keynote speaker at a large family camp and he asked me to go along with him. At the beginning of the night meeting, my usually punctual dad, was running a little late. I was sitting in the front row, waiting and looking for him, as hundreds of people milled around talking to each other. Suddenly I heard someone clear their throat with an "ahem." I knew it was my dad. I turned around and looked at the very back of the tabernacle, where he stood. People around me were making all kinds of noise but I had heard something familiar. It was my dad. How did I recognize him over all of that crowd? Because I knew his voice and I was listening for it.

I don't think I have ever desired anything more, than to have the ability to hear God's voice. Often in my prayers I would say to the Lord, "teach me how to hear your voice. Give me spiritual elephant ears so that I can easily hear you." I longed to have the relationship with God that the great men and women of the Bible had. I wanted to hear God speak to me like he did with Abraham, his friend. I wanted to experience what Moses experienced up on the mountain when God Almighty spoke. I wanted to hear God whisper to me in the valley and shout from the mountain tops like He did with David, Ezekiel and Elijah.

Longing for the ability to hear God has brought me on an amazing journey. I have learned to never underestimate the many ways that God may speak to me. One night, while living in West Africa, I awoke knowing that God had spoken to me in a dream. In my dream I saw the word "Kathryn." That name had been written in script letters and as the word was completed, I heard God speak. He said, "Pray for Kathryn, spelled with a **K**. She is in Sloan Kettering Hospital."
I had no other information. I didn't even know if there was a hospital called Sloan Kettering. Not only that, but I didn't know anyone by the name of Kathryn whose name started with a letter **K** instead of a **C**. I sent out emails asking if anyone had heard of a Sloan Kettering Hospital or of a Kathryn who needed prayer. No one responded. That dream stayed with me and, years later I found out that Sloan Kettering Hospital is indeed a real hospital in New York City. I still pray for Kathryn spelled with a **K**. Why do I do this? Because God said so, of course.

> There are countless ways God speaks but there is only one way to learn his voice. That way, is spending time with him and listening to him when

I have a friend who once told me how she had been awakened in the middle of the night, having had a dream that left her shaking. She saw her son running for his life, trying to escape someone who was chasing him with guns. In the dream she saw him running up to a stone wall and looking back seeing no way of escape. She knew God was speaking to her, telling her to pray so she stayed up all night praying for her son. The next morning he called her and told her how he had wandered into a very dangerous part of a city and had run away from street thugs chasing him with guns. He told her how he had come face to face with a stone wall. Just as he thought all was lost, someone from the other side of the wall, peeked over the top of the wall and reached out his hand. In what seemed like lightning speed, her son was pulled over the top, only to find that no one was there. God had sent an angel at the same time his mom had the dream.

I rarely have dreams that I remember. The dreams I do remember are usually very significant. I discovered years ago that if I am awakened by a dream, it is often God speaking to me. Dreams can provide a backdrop to visualize when God speaks. However, one should note that not all dreams are spiritual dreams. It takes time to develop the ability to differentiate between God's voice and a natural dream. Many people have anxiety dreams and others have nightmares. These dreams steal peace and often leave the dreamer all shook up. Satan knows how powerful dreams can be. It is for this reason that he uses tormenting dreams. Too often God's people, who have a spiritual gift of dreams, are tormented by evil dreams in order to steal their gift. Their spirit is open to dreams and Satan knows that if he can make them afraid of dreaming, he can take away their blessing. Then there are prophetic or revelation dreams. These dreams can be very impactful. They can be warnings or instruction. There is almost no end to the ways God can speak through dreams.

I have been privileged to hear God's voice many times and in different ways. Sometimes he has spoken to me in an audible voice and at other times he has so quietly whispered to my heart that, had I not been listening, I would have missed hearing him. There are countless ways God speaks but there is only one way to learn his voice. That way, is spending time with him and listening to him when he speaks.

John 6:45

"It is written in the prophets, And they shall be all taught of God. Every man therefore that hath heard, and hath learned of the Father, cometh unto me."

In **John 6:45** Jesus quoted the prophet Isaiah, and then made the conclusion that the only way we can come to Him is by hearing and learning of the Father. Learning, takes listening. God is looking for people who have an ear to hear Him because it is the only way we can truly find Jesus.

There is a big difference between hearing and listening. Hearing is something we do automatically. It takes no thought to hear. A sound happens and our ears pick up that sound. Our brain then registers that a sound was made. Listening, on the other hand, is making a conscious decision to focus on the sound we hear. God has a lot to say but often we aren't listening. Even though our ears may hear, we have not learned to listen or learned to practice the presence and voice of God; therefore we do not know it is Him when He does speak.

You may ask, what is practicing the presence of God? It is simply making a habit of spending time with God. It becomes our responsibility to learn how to hear His voice. The most important thing you can do is to make a habit of spending time with God. The more time you spend, the more God will speak. The more time you spend, the clearer He will sound to you. The more time you spend with Him, the less confusion you will feel.

In **Matthew 13**, Jesus explained why He spoke in parables. He said, those who hear and understand are given the mysteries of the Kingdom. It's like He is explaining, that those who have learned to listen or have practiced being in His presence, will understand what He is saying. They are the ones who can hear with their ears and understand in their heart. There are others who can not hear because their heart is hard. They haven't learned to listen. Even today, He is looking for people who not only hear with their ears, but understand what He is saying. What a wonderful blessing it is indeed, to hear and understand God's voice.

Matthew 13:10-16

"And the disciples came, and said unto him, Why speakest thou unto them in parables? He answered and said unto them, Because it is given unto you to know the mysteries of the kingdom of heaven, but to them it is not given... For this people's heart is waxed gross, and their ears are dull of hearing, and their eyes they have closed; lest at any time they should see with their eyes, and hear with their ears, and should understand with their heart, and should be converted, and I should heal them.

But blessed are your eyes, for they see: and your ears, for they hear. For verily I say unto you, That many prophets and righteous men have desired to see those things which ye see, and have not seen them; and to hear those things which ye hear, and have not heard them."

Hebrews 5:11

"Of whom we have many things to say, and hard to be uttered, seeing ye are dull of hearing."

Practicing God's voice is much like the time we spend with our family. I know my sister's voice and she knows mine. I can tell when she is in a room, just by listening for her voice. She can do the same with me. Not only do we know each other's voices, but we have the ability to differentiate between our voices and anyone else's in the room.

Many years ago, while I was living in Pennsylvania, I traveled to a small city with my friend Cathy. Our plan was to go to the mall and do some shopping. My sister lived a hour and a half from me and this city was somewhere in-between. I had no expectation that she would be anywhere near to where we were shopping because she worked weekdays. Cathy and I had decided to eat subs for lunch and we were telling stories and laughing. We were munching on our lunch, when my sister came running in. Imagine my surprise when she shouted, "I knew you were here. I just knew it. I heard you laughing all the way down the hall, almost to the other end of the mall." She heard me all right and there I was; right where my voice had led her.

> If you will spend time with Him and wait for Him to speak, He will. He won't disappoint you. He will speak and you will begin this wonderful journey of hearing and learning His voice.

How did she know I was in the mall? She knew, because she grew up with me and had years of experience listening to my voice. My sister Cheri, was able, with all the voices in the shopping mall, to lock onto my voice and know I was there. Listening is also how we learn to hear God's voice. If you will spend time with Him and wait for Him to speak, He will. He won't disappoint you. He will speak and you will begin this wonderful journey of hearing and learning His voice.

John 8:47

"Whoever is of God hears the words of God. The reason why you do not hear them is that you are not of God." ESV

One of the amazing things that happens when we spend time listening to God's voice is that it starts a transition in us and soon we begin to talk and eventually think like Him. Listening actually changes how we think and speak.

Genesis 1:27

"So God created man in his own image, in the image of God created he him; male and female created he them."

2 Corinthians 3:18

"But we all, with open face beholding as in a glass the glory of the Lord, are changed into the same image from glory to glory, even as by the Spirit of the Lord."

My husband Fred and I adopted our daughter Marie-Louise, when she was six and a half years old. She was born in the country of Cote d'Ivoire and spoke French when we got her. Through the years something amazing has happened. When people call our house and she answers the phone, many people think she is me. They can't tell the difference between her voice and mine. Even my own dad couldn't tell the difference. I was born in the United States and she in Africa. My native tongue is English and her's is French. But now, after many years together, we sound alike. Likewise when we spend time with God, He changes what we sound like. We even begin to sound like Him!

One day Marie-Louise came into my bedroom complaining about a video some visiting children were watching. She told me that she had changed the movie because it wasn't good for our little guests. I was shocked because that same movie was one she had tried to watch not too many years ago. We had a big fight over that same film when I told her she couldn't watch it. Now, she was talking and thinking like me.

Whenever I think about learning to hear God's voice I think about the prophet Samuel. He was just a little boy when he went to live with Eli the priest. Eli's two sons were also priests and very wicked. Eli did nothing to make them stop their evil practices. As a result God was not speaking to him anymore.

I Samuel 3:10

"And the LORD came and stood, calling as at other times, "Samuel! Samuel!" And Samuel said, "Speak, for your servant hears." ESV

When Samuel first moved in with Eli, he didn't know the voice of God. One night while he was sleeping, God called and said, "Samuel, Samuel." The little boy thought he had heard Eli calling. So, he ran to Eli and said, "Here I am." Realizing that it was God who was speaking to Samuel, the old man instructed Samuel to answer God. Just as the priest instructed, Samuel responded by saying, "Speak Lord for your servant is listening." This was the beginning of Samuel's remarkable relationship with God. He became the greatest prophet in all of history. He heard the words of God and spoke them. As a matter-of-fact, the Bible says that none of Samuel's words fell to the ground. This was to say that everything Samuel said was just and true. Whenever he spoke for God, his words were right on the mark. He had learned to hear God's voice, repeat what he had heard, and lead the people of God.

Revelation 2:17 addresses,"the one who has an ear to hear." We have all been given the ability to hear but not everyone has an ear to hear. Those who have an ear to hear are those who are tuned in and listen. God has a lot to say to those who are listening. Many people say they want to hear God's voice but not everyone wants to invest the time in learning to hear. It is much the same as learning to hear another language. When I first started living in West Africa, my French was almost nonexistent. I had learned some French in high school but my best French left me with only the ability to read a menu in a restaurant. I wanted to learn but I had to have a French ear to hear. It took a while but soon I was singing some songs in French. As I learned the meanings of the songs and started connecting the words to English, my ear for French greatly improved. After some more time, living in the presence of French speakers and trying to hear what they were saying, my French speaking improved. I have been traveling in the Philippines and just recently I discovered I am developing an ear to hear Tagalog. Spending time with the speaker and having a desire to understand, develops an ear to hear. It is the same way with God's voice. We need to develop ears that hear because God has a lot to say.

Today, there are many voices. No matter where you go, even in the farthest reaches of the world, there are radio waves, cell phones, faxes, satellite television and email. All of these have voices that can be heard and understood if you are tuned in. As I have traveled in Africa and Asia, I have been amazed at the amount of cell phones, iPods, iPads, and MP3 players I see. All over the world, voices compete with God for your attention. One question remains, what voice are you listening to?

There is no instant or quick way to learn the voice of God. It takes time to train our ears to hear. And it takes commitment to listen to Him, shutting out all other voices. We learn the voice of God, through prayer, reading and meditation on His word, and quieting our life so we can train our spiritual ears to hear.

A good radio receiver can lock-in to specific signals of radio waves and in turn broadcast clear messages from specific frequencies. When radio was new, the receivers were not as good as they are now. There were many conditions in which sound would drift in and out. Sometimes the signal would be completely lost. Atmospheric conditions most often disturbed radio receivers. Our son Chris, would wake up in the middle of cloudy nights to catch his favorite radio show as the sound waves skipped across the clouds. Now we have receivers that can lock-in and hold specific sounds. Cell phones, iPods, iPads, televisions, and satellites, to name a few, all have a receiver that can distinguish or lock onto one specific frequency. Have you ever wondered why it is that when you call someone's cell phone, only their phone recognizes the call? There is a specific receiver that locks it all in and holds onto the digital signature.

We are bombarded with sounds and voices, everyday. Sounds that frightened us as children (vacuum cleaners, loud trucks, or fireworks)

Because God Said So

no longer scare us because we have learned to distinguish between those sounds or voices and we learned to perceive that there is no reason to fear. Even though sounds and voices are all around us, God has given us the ability to distinguish between each and every one of them.

We need to practice, until we become tuned-in receivers so that we can distinguish between our own voice, the voice of others, the voice of Satan and the voice of God. There is no instant or quick way to learn the voice of God. It takes time to train our ears to hear. And it takes commitment to listen to Him, shutting out all other voices. We learn the voice of God, through prayer, reading and meditation on His word, and quieting our life so we can train our spiritual ears to hear. Those who are willing to invest themselves into that process will not only begin to hear God's voice, but their life will never be the same. *Because God Said So.*

Jeremiah 7:23

"But this thing commanded I them, saying, Obey my voice, and I will be your God, and ye shall be my people: and walk ye in all the ways that I have commanded you, that it may be well unto you." KJV

Hebrews 5:14

"But solid food is for the mature, who by constant use have trained themselves to distinguish good from evil..." ESV

Exodus 19:5-6

"Now therefore, if ye will obey my voice indeed, and keep my covenant, then ye shall be a peculiar treasure unto me above all people: for all the earth is mine: And ye shall be unto me a kingdom of priests, and an holy nation. These are the words which thou shalt speak unto the children of Israel."

17

Prayer

Lord Jesus, help me as I learn to hear your voice. I am so hungry to know you and hear what you are saying. My world is so busy and full of noise that sometimes your voice is drowned out. Lord, I know you have much to say to me and I want to hear. Give me ears to hear. Give me the ability to shut the world out and hear you. I can do this,

Because You Said So!

Chapter 2
A New Name

I have a lot of friends. Some are near to me and others far, but the one thing that is common among them all is the fun we have when we finally get together and can talk. Communication is key in great friendships. In Genesis 17 Abram, later known as Abraham, was the first man that God called His friend. They had a friendship forged from time invested in each other. That friendship also brought about a name change for Abram.

There were many times when Abram heard God speak. However, there is one special time that stands out. That would be the day that God told Abram that he would no longer be called Abram but Abraham. This is significant because the name Abraham means "Father of a Multitude." At this point in Abram's life, he had no children. Now, because of what God said; Abram would tell everyone around him that he was no longer Abram but Abraham, the father of multitudes. Every time he was called by that name he came into an agreement with God and his life began to reflect that transition. This would be laughable and perhaps downright ridiculous to his friends. Imagine the teasing that went on behind his back.

This was bad enough but God didn't stop there. He said that Abraham's wife Sari would no longer be called Sari but Sarah. God declared that Sarah would bare the promised covenant son and from her would come nations and kings of people. Sari the barren woman was now to be addressed as Sarah. Abraham and Sarah had to speak, in faith, according to what God had said. This wouldn't be so bad if it weren't for the fact that Abraham was almost 100 years old and Sarah almost 90. How much more laughable could it be than to insist that you were the Father of Multitudes at the ripe old age of 100 and that your barren 90 year old wife would bear nations?

Abraham came into agreement with God each time he spoke the new name of Sarah. Likewise Sarah, came into agreement with God, every time she called her husband Abraham. Doing this, they became what they said. Did this happen over night? No! But their lives truly changed all because God Said So.

Genesis 12:2

"And I will make of thee a great nation, and I will bless thee, and make thy name great; and thou shalt be a blessing:"

Of course God had a plan and the rest of the story is exciting as Sarah and Abraham do indeed have a child in their old age. His name was Isaac and from him a great nation was born. The word of the Lord was true. The word of the Lord, spoken to Abraham, created faith and hope in both Abraham and Sarah.

If it had not been for God's spoken word, it is doubtful that Abraham and Sarah in their old age, would have even tried to conceive a child. However, there was power in the words of God and as a result those words created. The authority of God's word forever changed the lives of Abraham and Sarah. Isaac was born, *Because God Said So*.

Names have meanings. My husband's name Fred, means peace. My name Deborah, means a fluttering bee or the one who pollinates. It is interesting that both of our names seem to describe us very well. While my husband is an awesome peacemaker and counselor, I am truly a fluttering bee. We have taken on the characteristics of those names.

> The authority of God's word forever changed the lives of Abraham and Sarah. Isaac was born, *Because God Said So*.

Galatians 3:6-9

"Even as Abraham believed God, and it was accounted to him for righteousness.
Know ye therefore that they which are of faith, the same are the children of Abraham. And the scripture, foreseeing that God would

justify the heathen through faith, preached before the gospel unto Abraham, saying, In thee shall all nations be blessed. So then they which be of faith are blessed with faithful Abraham."

One of the blessings God gave to Abraham was that God would make his name great. There was a promise attached to the name change. When we become close to someone and become their friends; they often change our name and those names also come with a promise. My husband may call me Deb or Debby but sometimes he also calls me names of affection, Honey or Sweetheart. Those names also come with a promise of love and endearment. In the same way, God changes our name and gives us the promise of love and affection.

Genesis 12:2-3

"And I will make of thee a great nation, and I will bless thee, and make thy name great; and thou shalt be a blessing: And I will bless them that bless thee, and curse him that curseth thee: and in thee shall all families of the earth be blessed. "

I have a friend in West Africa who was born into a family of animists. She had been given a name; but when she became a Christian that name became offensive to her. One day a prophet came to her and said, "God has changed your name. From this day forward you shall be called Esther. I personally, have never known her by any other name. She has always been Esther to me. Her life resembles that name too, as she is much like the Biblical Esther. She is truly one who has come to the Kingdom of God "For such a time as this." **(Esther 4:14)** She is a gifted translator, she pastors a church, and runs a girl's home. It is amazing what God does when He changes our name.

We should also consider Peter, who was often called by his other name, Simon. The name Simon means hearing or to listen. And Peter means a rock or pebble. It seems to me that as I read the stories of Peter, his name is truly symbolic of who he was. He wanted to be Simon the hearing one. He desired to hear the words of Jesus but so often he found himself stumbling as he listened and tried to do as Jesus said. I can just imagine what it was like as the dual-named man listened but sometimes his hearing was like speaking to a rock, or a stubborn hard headed man. He sometimes seemed so hard headed that one wonders, as his life unfolds, if he would ever understand what Jesus was teaching him. And yet he kept coming back to Jesus for more to hear. As I read the early stories of Simon Peter's life, I noticed something very significant. Almost all of the time Peter is referred to as Peter or Simon Peter however, in the last chapter of the book of John where Jesus asks Peter if he loves him, Jesus uses the name Simon. He no longer referred to Peter the hard head but Simon the hearing one. Peter was changing and Jesus used the name that now best fit the person.

I Peter 2:9-10

"But ye are a chosen generation, a royal priesthood, an holy nation, a peculiar people; that ye should shew forth the praises of him who hath called you out of darkness into his marvellous light: Which in time past were not a people, but are now the people of God: which had not obtained mercy, but now have obtained mercy."

We can't forget Barnabas as we look at names that change. (**Acts 4:36**) He is an interesting character who was never called by his real name, it was Joseph. As a matter of fact, the only reason Joseph was called Barnabas, was because he was always encouraging and helping people in their faith. He was an encourager and his new name Barnabas, meant encourager or son of comfort. His name changed as people began to call him as he was, an encourager. What if we began to refer to ourselves by the names that God calls us? What if people started calling us names that reflected our personality? Would you be known as Blessing, Peace, or Hope? Or would you be known like an old Sesame Street character Oscar the Grouch?

There is an old song we used to sing at church when I was a little girl. It went like this. "There's a new name written down in glory and it's mine, oh yes it's mine." When we come to Jesus, one of the first things He does is make us His friend and change our name. Jesus says, in the book of Revelation, that we have been given a new name, written in stone. Written in stone? What an amazing thought. It's not easy to write on stone, but once a name is carved in stone it stays for a very long time. Stones symbolize permanence. Have you ever noticed that most old grave markers are engraved in stone? The name written in stone will last for many many generations to come, some for thousands of years. When Jesus says He will write our new name in stone He says that to indicate that it is an everlasting new name.

> What better way to fully understand the power and plan of God than to defeat and conquer the voices of discouragement with ears that hear when God Almighty speaks.

Yes
We also see a position connected to the new name promised, in **Revelation 2:17**. It says that the new name is given to the one who hears what the Spirit is saying and also to the one who conquers. What better way to fully understand the power and plan of God than to defeat and conquer the voices of discouragement with ears that hear when God Almighty speaks.

Revelation 2:17

"He that hath an ear, let him hear what the Spirit saith unto the churches; To him that overcometh will I give to eat of the hidden manna, and will give him a white stone, and in the stone a new name written, which no man knoweth saving he that receiveth *it*."

Revelation 3:12

"Him that overcometh will I make a pillar in the temple of my God, and he shall go no more out: and I will write upon him the name of my God, and the name of the city of my God, [which is] new Jerusalem, which cometh down out of heaven from my God: and *I will write upon him* my new name. "

Our daughter Marie-Louise, had several names when we first adopted her. Her first name was confusing because her cousins and friends called her one name but her birth certificate had another name. Her middle name was Marie-Louise and so we kept that and then changed her last name to Davis. We wanted everyone to know that she was our daughter. Her name needed to reflect the new family name and end the confusion of her first name.

When we were considering adopting Marie-Louise, we emailed our son Chris and asked him what he thought about us adopting a little girl. Without having seen the little girl he replied, " All my life I have wanted a sister. Yes take her." He even went so far as to say, "If anything happens to you and dad, I want her. I will take care of her."

Marie-Louise didn't have a mom and dad. She was alone. Then she became a member of our family. Everyone of our friends and family welcomed her and wanted her.

In **Psalms 68:6**, the Bible says that God takes the lonely and puts them into families. Imagine, if one day, at the beginning of time, God the father, went to his son Jesus and said, "I have found someone who I would like to adopt into our family."....Jesus replied, " All of my life I have wanted brothers and sisters...not only do I want them, but I will take care of them forever."

No matter who you are when you come to Jesus, your name changes, from Lost to Found, Sick to Healed, Angry to Happy, Rejected to Loved, Condemned to Forgiven, Abandoned to Accepted.

Because of the blood of Jesus, we are adopted in the family of God. Now we are sons and daughters of Abraham. Abraham's blessings are now our blessings. We have also become the friend of God. This means that the promise, to make Abraham's name great, applies to us too. Our name is now great. Why? Because God said so. That's why!

Romans 9:8

"That is, They which are the children of the flesh, these are not the children of God: but the children of the promise are counted for the seed."

Galatians 4:7

"Wherefore thou art no more a servant, but a son; and if a son, then an heir of God through Christ."

Not only has God made our new name great but it is a reflection of who we really are in Christ. We were all born with natural names. Our moms and dads picked out a name that they liked and attached it to us. As we grow older we also take on new names. Perhaps you are always singing and whistling while you work. Your friends may call you Happy or Song Bird. Maybe you are a grouch and everyone calls you, That Grumpy Old Man, or Scrooge. No matter who you are when you come to Jesus, your name changes, from Lost to Found, Sick to Healed, Angry to Happy, Rejected to Loved, Condemned to Forgiven, Abandoned to Accepted. The blood of Jesus changes every part of who we are. It even makes our name great. You may ask, how does this happen? It happens, *Because God said so*.

Hosea..1:9

"Then said *God*, Call his name Loammi: for ye *are* not my people, and I will not be your *God*."

Hosea 2:23

"And I will sow her unto me in the earth; and I will have mercy upon her that had not obtained mercy; and I will say to *them which were* not my people, Thou *art* my people; and they shall say, *Thou art* my God.'"

Prayer

Lord Jesus, thank you for giving me a new name. Help me to realize that I am loved and accepted by you. Help me to remember that with your help, I can change. Lord change my name like you did for Barnabas. Make my name a reflection of what you have done in my life. I know you can do this,

Because You Said So!

Chapter 3
Direction

People have asked me, "How do I know if I am in God's will?" Or, "How do I know what direction I should go in? I feel like God wants me to do something but I am just not sure if it is something I dreamed up or if it is God speaking to me." I would never presume to have perfect direction however the old adage, "It is easier to steer a moving ship than one that is standing still" is very true. Have you ever thought about that? When a ship is moving through the waters, you can move the rudder and the ship turns but when the ship is standing still, you may try to move the rudder but it won't make any difference. The boat won't change direction because it isn't moving, it's anchored down. Life can be like that. If you are not moving, or trying to accomplish what God has given you to do, than He can't change your direction. It's like being stuck in the mud. You will be going nowhere.

In **Genesis 24** we see an amazing story unfold as Abraham sends his servant back to his family. He instructs him to find a wife for his son Isaac. The servant, arriving in the general area of Abraham's relatives, asked God to give him a sign about which girl would be right for his master's son. While sitting by a well, he would ask a girl to give him a drink from her jug. If the girl was the right girl for his master's son, then the girl would respond that she would indeed give him a drink and also water his camels too. The servant had traveled with ten camels and a camel could drink twenty to thirty gallons of water in just a few minutes. That would amount to about 250 gallons of water that the girl would have to draw by hand from the well. This was almost an impossible request however, the servant of Abraham didn't want to make any mistake and bring the wrong girl home to Isaac.

Genesis 24:27

"And he said, Blessed *be* the LORD God of my master Abraham, who hath not left destitute my master of his mercy and his truth: I *being* in the way, the LORD led me to the house of my master's brethren. "

Abraham's servant, traveling throughout the land of Abraham's forefathers, may have stopped at many wells by the time this part of the story is told. When he arrived at this particular well, he asked a very beautiful girl by the name of Rebekah, for a drink. She responded in just the right way as to indicate that she was God's choice. After she finished drawing 250 gallons of water, he asked the girl who she was. She began to tell him of her family; indicating that she was indeed a relative of Abraham's. The servant then bowed his head and began to worship the Lord, declaring that, "I being in the way, the Lord led me."

If we have honestly decided to listen and trust God, then we can't miss the plan of God. God Himself said that He would lead us. God wants you to succeed..

Sometimes God just gives us a small part of information as to what direction we should go. This servant of Abraham had been given only one piece of information. "Go back to the land of Abraham's family." As he was faithful to step-out in faith and start moving in that direction, God revealed another piece of information. Had the man never started on his journey or had never arrived at that well, he would have never met Rebekah. Some people never seem to go anyplace in their life and wonder why they can't see God's plan for them. The key, to understanding God's will, begins with the first step. From there on, and with each continued step, the Lord will give direction.

Isaiah 30:21

"And thine ears shall hear a word behind thee, saying, This *is* the way, walk ye in it, when ye turn to the right hand, and when ye turn to the left.l."

Therefore my answer to those looking for direction, usually begins with, "Keep doing what God has put in your hand to do and when He wants you to move He will move you." Lets look back on the story of Abraham's servant. Had he never gone to Mesopotamia he never would have found Rebecca. She was God's choice. However the servant had to start traveling, looking as he went. That's when he found her. It really is that easy. God wants to direct us and he doesn't want us to live in confusion. So often people assume that God is silent and that He just expects us to make the right decisions. Then, if we make a mistake, fail, or go in the wrong direction He is ready to beat us. That is not God's way. He is a loving and good Father. He is not looking for ways to trip us up or to see us fail. No he is lovingly guiding us, one step at a time.

Matthew 7:7

"Ask, and it shall be given you; seek, and ye shall find; knock, and it shall be opened unto you."

A loving father instructs his child in the way he should go and even gives lots of direction. Should his child start to go in a bad direction or make mistakes, the father, then instructs his child and helps him along. **Isaiah 30:21** tells us that God is like that, directing us in the way we should go. If we have honestly decided to listen and trust God, then we can't miss the plan of God. God Himself said that He would lead us. God wants you to succeed. He doesn't want you to fail. He will give you direction along the way, just when you need it. Trusting in God's direction is always safe. As you walk with Him, He steers you in the right way. It is impossible to go wrong when we listen to His voice. Why? *Because God Said So*.

Psalms 1:6a

"For the Lord watches over the path of the godly,"

I have often thought about Moses and his life as a shepherd. He was a man who had been raised in Pharaoh's home, and when he became older he found out that he was a Hebrew. That information changed everything for Moses. Imagine the thoughts and questions that flooded his mind. Because he had been raised in the home of the King of Egypt, he had every advantage and every blessing he could ever want.

When he found out who he really was, he was no longer comfortable with his old life. Surely he felt out of place. He must have wondered about his life and why he alone was spared, when other Hebrew babies, born when he had been born, died. Did God spare him for a special purpose? Could God use him, because of his special upbringing or his place in the land of Egypt? Moses' story started in the palace, however because of his temper, Moses killed an Egyptian and became a wanted man. He fled the land of Egypt, leaving behind the only life that he knew.

Moses later married a woman in the desert land and he took care of her father's sheep. For an Egyptian man to take care of sheep was humiliating. Never would an Egyptian be satisfied by taking care of sheep, and most certainly not a royal Egyptian. However this is where Moses found himself. Everyday he watched the sheep. He cleaned the sheep. He fed the sheep. He led the sheep in fresh pastures. Moses carried the wounded sheep around his neck and would fight any wild animal that would try to devour his sheep.

Have you ever wondered what was going on in his mind, as day after day he plodded on in a dead-end job. Did he question if God could ever use him? Did he wonder why his life was spared and if he had blown his one and only chance to do what God had called him to do? I know these would be the questions I would ask. Could God ever have another, perhaps better plan for Moses? After all, he was out in the desert going no-where fast. And yet day after day, Moses was faithful doing what he was supposed to be doing. Day after day he died to himself, serving his father-in-law, doing a job he probably hated. Day after day, he showed up and cared for those little animals until one day God spoke to him and his whole life changed.

Exodus 3:4

"And when the LORD saw that he turned aside to see, God called unto him out of the midst of the bush, and said, Moses, Moses. And he said, Here am I."

All of those years of faithful shepherding came to a climax as God began to instruct Moses. He would show this, now humble man, how to bring God's people out of bondage and into the land of promise.

God needed an educated man, a man who could talk to Pharaoh, a man who knew how to address the royalty of Egypt and who understood their protocol. All of these would be something that would have been second nature for one raised in the house of Pharaoh. God needed a man who could lead the Hebrews out of Egypt. He was also looking for a man who had patience and mercy for the people of God, skills that Moses had learned all of those years taking care of sheep. Moses had learned to love the unlovely and had learned how to protect and lead his stubborn flock, not so unlike the Hebrews he would rescue from Egypt. Moses was a faithful man, even in the midst of his trials, and now his life had taken a new turn.

Luke 16:10

"He that is faithful in that which is least is faithful also in much: and he that is unjust in the least is unjust also in much."

God would not have used Moses had he not become a faithful servant. His faithfulness prepared him for the next step. It was in this desert time, while Moses learned the life of a shepherd, that God spoke to him saying, "Take off your shoes. Don't come any closer. This is Holy Ground. I have heard the cries of my people in Egypt. Go and speak to Pharaoh and bring my people out of Egypt." Why was it Holy Ground? *Because God Said So*! Why should Moses speak to Pharaoh? And why would Moses be the one to bring God's people out of Egypt? *Because God Said So*, of course!

Moses was full of questions, so much so, that God got a little impatient with him. "What should I say? Who should I say sent me? What happens if Pharaoh says no?" God humored all of Moses' questions but the bottom line was, "Go! Because I, the Great I Am, said so!" And you know what happened? Moses went to Egypt. He spoke to Pharaoh. He did the signs and wonders that God had told him to do. He led the Hebrews through the plagues and Pharaoh's false promises. Over and over he promised that they could leave and then always, he changed his mind. Finally the last plague came and out from Egypt went the people of Abraham, Isaac and Jacob. They all followed Moses, young and old alike. They didn't really know where they were going. but God directed them with a pillar of fire by night and cloud by day. God opened the Red Sea and drowned their enemies. Why did all these things happen? Because God said they would!

God told Moses all of these things before they happened and because God said so, Moses acted. I don't think Moses ever wanted to go back to Egypt. Perhaps he thought that everything Egypt had for him was lost forever. Yet God had a plan to take him back to the very place he had run away from. The Almighty was faithful to direct Moses because Moses was willing to listen to what God said. Moses was faithful to what God had given him to do and he did it all, *Because God Said So*.

After several years of living in the Ivory Coast, Fred and I began to realize that God was moving us on to a new place. An old woman came to our Bible school and told Fred that the Lord had a word for me. Fred brought her to our house and she began to tell me what the Lord had told her. She started with, "I know you don't want to do this, but you are going to be sent back to America. God has a plan for you and it won't happen if you don't go." Well, the last thing I wanted to do was to leave the Ivory Coast. I loved being a missionary and just the thought of being based out of the USA was unpleasant. I believed that God had a plan and as much as I didn't want to leave, I also didn't want to miss out on this special plan God had for me.

As I was packing up my things, to take with me or give away, God began to speak. He told me that he would give me a house back in the USA. He also gave me ideas for books to write. My life was changing even as I packed my bags. Like Moses, I questioned God. I asked the Lord what the plan was. I also asked Him why I had to leave. The only answer was, "*Because I said so*." I still don't know all of the reasons why we had to leave the Ivory Coast (besides the obvious civil-war). I haven't seen all of the plan that God has promised. But I did get a house in New York State. I have written several books and plan to write more. Every day God opens doors that amaze me. God's plan unfolds piece by piece as I walk with him. *Because He Said So*.

Psalms 119:105

"Thy word *is* a lamp unto my feet, and a light unto my path. ."

I never could have happily, left my home in West Africa, had I not had that word from God. On difficult days, when it seems like the promise is nowhere in sight, I remind myself, and God, by saying, "God, you said you have a plan. You told me to settle in New York. God, this was your idea, not mine." As I ponder over the words that God has spoken to me, both in my own heart and through the mouth of others, my faith is renewed and my eyes are opened. I see the hand of God on my life and I feel His presence in ways I have never felt before. He promised me that His word would be a light illuminating my path. As long as I stayed in the light of his word, I know that I will always remain in His will.

John 8:32

"And ye shall know the truth, and the truth shall make you free."

The Bible tells us that knowing the truth will set us free. I like to remind myself of the promises God has given me. God's word is truth. However, truth alone does not set us free. We have to 'know' the truth. No one can be set free by truth alone. We have to know it. That word "know" means to understand or become intimately acquainted with. As we meditate on God's word, we become intimately acquainted with what he has to say. That knowledge, or understanding, builds faith and eventually sets us free. We are free because fear of the future is no longer an issue. We now have faith for our future. Fear of the unknown has no place in our hearts became we are consumed with God's word and we know God, even as He now knows us. Like the prophet Jeremiah, we can realize that we have a hope and a future.

> As we meditate on God's word, we become intimately acquainted with what he has to say. That knowledge, or understanding, builds faith and eventually sets us free.

Jeremiah 29:11

"For I know the plans I have for you," declares the LORD, "plans to prosper you and not to harm you, plans to give you hope and a future."

So what does this mean to you and me today? It means that, if we are faithful doing what we know to do, we can be sure that God will speak and direct us when it is time for us to move on. It means that, like

Moses, you may feel like you are in a desert place but you have hope. The desert will not last forever. Don't allow the devil to steal your peace, your joy and your faith. God will speak and when He does; be prepared to listen. Everything will change, just *Because He Said So*!

Prayer
Lord Jesus, I need your wisdom and direction. Plan my days and take away the fears that I have been consumed with. Lord I trust you with my life. I know you have good plans for me. Help me to rest in you when life seems to be out of control. I know that I need not be afraid because you love me and you are directing my steps. I believe, Because You Said So!

Chapter 4
Favor

Psalms 30:7

"O Lord, in your good favor you made me secure."

Psalms 5:12

"For thou, LORD, wilt bless the righteous; with favour wilt thou compass him as *with* a shield."

Psalm 41:11

"By this I know that thou favourest me, because mine enemy doth not triumph over me."

Some of my favorite stories in the Bible center around the life of David. I often picture in my mind what he looked like. I even try to imagine his expressions. For example, the day the prophet Samuel came to David's home looking for the next king of Israel, was one I don't think David would ever forget. The shock and surprise on his face would have been a "photo op" or "selfie moment" had there been cameras and iPhones available that day. Rushing from the field and leaving his special little lambs with another, David's mind would have been a flurry of questions. "Why does the prophet want me? What have I done? Am I in some kind of trouble?" But nonetheless, David came. Why? Because the prophet said so.

Acts 13:22

"And when he had removed him, he raised up unto them David to be their king; to whom also he gave testimony, and said, I have found David the *son* of Jesse, a man after mine own heart, which shall fulfil all my will."

Arriving at his home, David stood before Samuel.
The prophet took out his horn of oil and proceeded to pour it all over the young shepherd. Everyone knew what this meant. David was being anointed King instead of King Saul. Saul had rejected God and so God rejected him. By God's own word, Saul was replaced by a special man whose heart ran hard after God.

I always felt very special whenever I was with my grandfather. One day my grandpa asked my sister and me, (I was probably 5 or 6 years old and my sister a year younger) to go to town with him. Of course the answer was yes. It always meant a treat of some sort whenever we went with him. This day was no exception. I can remember, that when we arrived at the local hardware store, my grandpa picked up the two of us girls and sat us on the counter. He chatted with the owner of the store and went on and on about how cute we were. I can still hear him say, "Aren't these just the cutest little girls you have ever seen?" Then he asked us if we wanted a piece of gum or candy from the barrel of sweets that the man had next to his cash register. Oh my eyes lit up as did my sister's. Yes we would love a piece of candy.

The man looked at me and then at my sister and said, "Well, Miff (my grandfather's name was Milford but his friends called him Miff) for two girls as nice as you say these are, they should have more than just a piece of candy. I'll give them the whole barrel. The whole barrel? I could hardly believe it was true. The giant barrel, equally as big as my sister or I, filled to the top with candy and bazooka bubblegum was going home with us. My grandpa said we were cute and because he said so, the hardware man thought so too.

I don't remember how long that barrel of candy lasted, but my mom said it took a long time to chew up all the bubble gum. Why did we bring all that gum and candy home? Because the man at the store said so! Grandpa's words of favor for me and my sister, influenced the

36

owner of the hardware shop. God's words of favor for David, spoken to the prophet Samuel, impacted a nation. Why? *Because God said so.*

Psalms 103:10-12

"He hath not dealt with us after our sins; nor rewarded us according to our iniquities. He does not deal with us as our sins deserve; he does not repay us as our misdeeds deserve. For as the heaven is high above the earth, so great is his mercy toward them that fear him. For as the skies are high above the earth, so his loyal love towers over his faithful followers. As far as the east is from the west, so far hath he removed our transgressions from us."

God wants everyone to know that He favors them. No one is left out and we all have the opportunity to live a life of favor. Why? Because He said so.

So many people never succeed in life, never accomplish what their life was meant to be, because no one ever spoke words of favor over them. Words are powerful and instead of favorable words many have been cursed with words of condemnation, hatred and fear. But these are not the words that God has spoken. God says in His word that as far as the east is from the west, so far has He removed our transgressions. He has granted us freedom, peace, and forgiveness. He wants us to be blessed and not cursed. He desires us to know that, as far as He is concerned, we are just the most wonderful person in all of His creation. Like my Grandfather, God is bragging about you. Don't let the devil close your ears and miss what God is saying about you.

One day my sister Cheri, had a conversation with God and He told her she was his favorite person. "How can that be?" she asked. With all the people in the world, how could she be God's favorite? God replied, "Everyone is my favorite!" Wow, that's hard to believe and even harder to understand. How can we all be God's favorite? How does that work? God wants everyone to know that He favors them. No one is left out and we all have the opportunity to live a life of favor. Why? Because He said so.

Psalms 30:5

"For his anger *endureth but* a moment; in his favour *is* life: weeping may endure for a night, but joy *cometh* in the morning."

In **Psalm 30**, we can see that even when we mess up, even if we fail, God's displeasure is only for a moment. It is just like a child with good parents. If the child does something wrong, it doesn't make his parents unhappy with him forever. No! The parents will discipline the child but it never changes the child's most favored status. Neither is God, our Heavenly Father, displeased forever but only for a short time. When we come to Him and express our sorrow, forgiveness comes like a flood and His favor washes away the failure. We have been given an awesome gift of favor that covers all of our insecurities. If we could just wrap our brain around this idea, our fear, panic and worry would just flee away. We have favor and not just any favor but favor that lasts a lifetime, that overcomes the past, and gives us a hope and a future. Why you may ask? Because God said so!

Jeremiah 29:11

"For I know the plans I have for you, declares the LORD, plans for welfare and not for evil, to give you a future and a hope.." ESV

God spoke to Jeremiah and told him that He had great plans for him. He told him that His plans were good plans and full of hope. There are people today who have no hope. Even when they read the Word of God and know that God has spoken to them, they still have no hope. Why? Because someone spoke hopelessness over them. They carry the words of the past, spoken by human people, as if those words have greater power than those of Almighty God. Soon these negative words are no longer the words of another but, they become an inner-dialogue that the hopeless person speaks in his own heart everyday. Those words of defeat, become like a wall of iron around their heart. Even when faced with the truth, they struggle to hear it. They repeat the words of condemnation louder and louder in their mind. Those words of death now become a part of their personality. How does this happen? Because someone said so.

Perhaps someone spoke curse words over you. Perhaps those word curses have attacked your very soul and have caused you to struggle daily, trying to defeat them. These curses come with words like these, "You are worthless. You will never amount to anything. No one will ever love you. You are fat and ugly. If you don't lose weight no one will ever want you. Just look at the way you dress, you will never get a good job. I can't believe you, why you are nothing but a good for nothing failure. You're so stupid and lazy, why did I ever marry you? If you marry him, you will be poor your whole life, he's nothing but a loser. You are nothing but a big disappointment to me." These kinds of words wrap themselves around your heart and choke the very life out of you. Before long you begin to say those same words to yourself everyday, self condemning yourself to a life of failure and hopelessness. "If I don't hope for something," you think, "then I won't be disappointed." We should not forget, that we often become what we say. Sometimes we even become what others say about us.

Oh

> Destructive words are nothing but lies and curses that have been aimed at you to keep you from the life of favor God has created for you.

Destructive words are nothing but lies and curses that have been aimed at you to keep you from the life of favor God has created for you. Our Heavenly Father has planned good for you. He loves you unconditionally. There is nothing that you can do that will separate you from His love. Like Jeremiah, God has good plans for you. He has a future for you and a life full of favor.

Romans 8:38-39

"For I am convinced that neither death, nor life, nor angels, nor heavenly rulers, nor things that are present, nor things to come, nor powers, nor height, nor depth, nor anything else in creation will be able to separate us from the love of God in Christ Jesus our Lord."

Paul tells us in the book of Romans, that nothing can separate us from the love of God. Did you catch that? Nothing can separate you from the love of God; not your sins, your failure, your looks, not someone else's word curse, nothing! However, before you can start walking in the favor of God you have to believe what God said. Remember that Jesus said the truth would set us free. The power of the truth will set you free if you can know it. You have to know who you are in Christ. You have to know who you are as a child of God. You have to know your position in the kingdom of God. You have to have an intimate understanding that what God says about you is true. Own the truth. Make it your own. Knowing these things makes you free indeed.

John 8:32

"...you will know the truth, and the truth will set you free." ESV

Just because other people don't know who you are in Christ, doesn't change who you are. The only person who can change your position is you! You shall know the truth and it will set you free. You are free. Don't listen to the lies spoken about you.

Several years ago, I started having some annual ladies meetings at my dad's church. Every year I would decorate and try to do something special at the church in preparation for the weekend ladies gathering. There was this one place in the church building that always bothered me. It was a flat ledge about seven feet high in the hallway next to the dining room. It was over a staircase going down to the basement floor but in the entrance of the dining room this ledge just looked like a sore spot to me. I wanted to put something decorative up there with some twinkle lights.

For several years I had asked different ones to put in an electrical outlet so I could plug in my lights. Every year I would return and there would be no outlet. After a few years, armed with a crowbar and the knowledge that that ledge was about to be taken out in favor of a lift, I climbed up on the ledge and proceeded to knock a hole in the wall so I could run an extension cord through to the adjoining room.

I had been traveling a lot with my husband, doing mission work in West Africa, and as a result I was gone for months at a time. New people would come to my dad's church and they wouldn't know who I was. On the day that I took up my crowbar and started banging on the wall, a man came up to me and not knowing who I was said, "Hey! You can't do that! What do you think you are doing?" In all fairness to him, he didn't know who I was, and he surely didn't expect a complete stranger to start knocking a hole in the wall.

I responded to him, "What do you mean I can't do this? I am the one with the crowbar. Besides, do you know who I am?"

He just looked at me like I was some kind of crazy woman. Finally I said, "Hi, I'm pastor Charley's daughter." I knew who I was and I also had that inside information about the ledge being taken down. I had authority because of whose daughter I was. Just because that man didn't know my identity, didn't change my position.

Just because other people don't know who you are in Christ, doesn't change who you are. The only person who can change your position is you! You shall know the truth and it will set you free. You are free. Don't listen to the lies spoken about you. We have all been created in the image of God. We are all beautiful. We all have the opportunity to succeed. God can, and does, take our failures and He makes them into successes. Nothing can separate us from His love. There is a future for you. You can hope again. You can believe for good things because God has promised them to you. You don't have to live your life, living out the word curses spoken against you.

The book of Proverbs tells us that when we live a life pleasing to the Lord, that even our enemies will be at peace with us. Imagine, having peace in every direction, in every area of your life. This amazing peace is a sign of God's favor.

King David, whose story can be found in **1st and 2nd Samuel,** enjoyed this special favor with God for his entire life. He messed up. He sinned. He made God angry and yet none of these things changed his position with God. Favor is not dependent on how good we are or how much we do for God. The favor of God is unconditional and forever. You don't have to be afraid anymore. Like David, you too can enjoy most favored status. Why? Because God said so!

Proverbs 16:7

"When a man's ways please the LORD, he maketh even his enemies to be at peace with him."

Prayer

Lord Jesus, I need hope today. I know you have promised me favor and that you love me unconditionally but Lord sometimes I forget. Remind me that you love me. Fill me with hope and give me your peace. I will believe that you love me and that I have most favored status,

Because You Said So!

Chapter 5
Hope

In **Acts 16 t**he Apostle Paul wanted to preach the Word of God throughout Asia but for some reason, God prevented him from doing so. He ended up in Troy wondering what to do, when he had a vision of a man from Macedonia. In the dream the man said, "Come to Macedonia (a region of Greece) and help us." Believing God had spoken to Paul, he and Silas changed their plans and boarded a ship bound for Greece. Upon arriving, Paul began to preach the Good News of Jesus' life, death and resurrection. A woman by the name of Lydia opened her heart to the "Good News" and she and her household became born again; changing their lives forever.

The next day as Paul and Silas were walking through town a demon possessed slave girl began to follow them and taunt them. After awhile Paul couldn't take it any more and commanded the evil spirits to leave the girl alone. There were some unscrupulous men in the town who used the girl, taking advantage of her demonic "gifting" of fortune telling. Unfortunately for them, she was now set free from the demons and couldn't tell fortunes anymore. Realizing the girl could no longer make money for them, they turned their anger on Paul and Silas. Accusing Paul of causing trouble in the city, the men had the two missionaries put into prison.

2 Corinthians 1:10

"He delivered us from such a deadly peril, and he will deliver us. On him we have set our hope that he will deliver us again.,"ESV

I would imagine that Paul could have been a little troubled if not downright confused and frustrated. He traveled to Macedonia only because God said so. Now he was in a prison for setting a young girl free, doing what apostles do. Others would have cried and accused God of making a mistake but not Paul. He and Silas knew they were in the right place. They had changed their plans because God said so. If God said so, then He had a plan and that was good enough for Paul. He and Silas began to pray and sing. They were worshiping the Lord when a great earthquake shook the prison and broke off their chains. The jailer was afraid because if even one prisoner escaped, he would pay with his life. Knowing that no one would willingly stay in a prison when the chains were broken off and the doors were all open, the hopeless jailor decided it would be best to kill himself, saving himself from possible torture that would surely precede his death. Suddenly, Paul spoke up and told him that no one had left and that God had good news for him. After Paul preached that good news, the jailor and his whole family were saved. This one event changed the life of a hopeless man. It quite possibly changed the lives of everyone in that jail.

It is interesting, that because Paul and Silas responded to the plan of God, both the Jailor and Lydia were saved along with their families. We don't always know why God takes us to different places but when we respond to His call, we can have confidence that God has a plan for our lives. Even if we don't understand God's reasons, even if the situation does not seem good or fair..we go. *Because God said so.*

We don't always know why God takes us to different places but when we respond to His call, we can have confidence that God has a plan for our lives.

Romans 8:28

"And we know that all things work together for good to them that love God, to them who are the called according to his purpose."

My husband had an invitation to teach in a Bible school in the Far East of Russia. He is not the happiest flyer but he knew God had spoken to him about going to Russia. So he packed his bags; just because God said so. After spending a few weeks in the Bible school, Fred felt a

deep connection grow between him, the ministry and the students. Giving no regard to his dislike for flying, he made plans to return and teach again. After his second trip, we knew that God had a future for us in Russia. We made plans to move to the Bible school as their new directors.
I was so excited to move to Russia. I have always been excited about new countries and our first mission trip to Guatemala only made me even more anxious to do mission work. I couldn't wait to go. We had been pastoring a church in Pennsylvania and loved our people but we knew God had spoken. We gave the church our six month notice and made plans to move to Russia. When the day finally arrived, we stored a few things in my mom and dad's attic, gave away most everything else, sold our house, and sent our son to Bible school.

Arriving at the school was a bit of a shock. The Bible school had moved and wasn't in the same location Fred had visited before. Now, it was located a ways from town, in a secluded spot, had no heat, no electricity, and no running water...well we did have some electricity, that is when we could connect a very long extension cord from a neighbor to the school.

After one week we found out that the local pastor had never correctly registered the Bible school after the school moved. Not only that, but some of the students didn't have the right papers for them to be there either. After one short week, we found ourselves being ushered away to our room by one of our students while the police searched the campus and arrested everyone. God in his great mercy protected us and we were never found. However, after just two short weeks, after we had sold all for this mission field, we found ourselves on a flight back to the USA.

Our house had been sold. Our ministry had been given to another. Our beloved son was gone to school and we had almost nothing. The one thing we did have, was the knowledge that the reason we went, was because God said so. We didn't know why things didn't turn out the way we had planned. We didn't know what we were supposed to do next; but we knew why we had gone. *Because God had said so.*

Hebrews 6:19

"We have this hope as an anchor for the soul, sure and steadfast, which reaches inside behind the curtain." ESV

Family, friends and prayer warriors encouraged us, telling us not to worry. No, we didn't make a mistake in going to Russia. However, there were times when we wondered, how could it be in the plan of God for us to go to Russia and have it all turn out the way it did. I have to confess, I cried the whole flight home. I wasn't very happy to be leaving Russia like this. There was one thing that I knew for sure. God would somehow make it all right. I had nothing to fear. Even if all was lost, the one thing I had, was the hope that I had in the Lord. He was the anchor of my soul. He was sure and steadfast. I could depend upon Him. He had never let me down. I could face my tomorrows because of Him.

While we were returning to the USA, my dad was making phone calls to a friend of his, a pastor in West Africa. Would he like to have some missionaries come and work with him? Of course the pastor said yes. Just a few short months later we found ourselves on another flight. Only this time, traveling to Africa. When we arrived we started a Bible school that was effective beyond our wildest imagination. Now, almost twenty years later, I see the wisdom and plan of God. We have students and graduates all over West Africa, Europe and even a few have become missionaries to the United States and Canada. Africa had never been in our plan. We went to Russia because God said so. And somehow in that wonderful way that God does, He took our disappointment and our faithfulness, and gave us spiritual sons and daughters in another land that we never dreamed we would have.

I don't think Paul and Silas anticipated having a revival in their prison however, they obeyed God and went to Macedonia...just *Because God Said So*. I never dreamed while traveling to Russia, that I would someday have a ministry in Africa. But it happened... all *Because God Said So*.

Life doesn't always go the way we plan. Teenagers enter university with dreams of an exciting future and something happens and life doesn't turn out the way they thought it would. Couples enter marriage with stars in their eyes dreaming of their future only to wake up one day and realize that their marriage didn't turn out as they had hoped and dreamed. People start new jobs thinking that it is a dream come true when all of a sudden they find themselves in a dead-end job going nowhere fast. Sickness, financial difficulties, family problems and accidents, steal the life and joy from many; leaving them hopeless and depressed. Maybe that someone is you.

Perhaps you have found yourself wondering if you made a mistake. Did you marry the wrong person? Did you take the wrong job? Did you get the wrong education? Is life a disappointment for you? Have you awakened only to discover that you hate your life and don't know how to make it right? Is all of your hope gone and you don't know what to do? Perhaps you should take a lesson from Paul and Silas and start praising the Lord in the midst of your brokenness.

I Thessalonians 5:18

"In everything give thanks. For this is God's will for you in Christ Jesus."

The Apostle Paul obviously found the secret to making disappointments turn into blessings. He told the church in Thessalonica that they should give thanks to God in every situation. This advice came from Paul's own life experiences. When he was in a bad situation and didn't know what to do, he gave thanks, praising the Lord, because He knew that God would make everything right. Sometimes giving thanks from a grateful heart is the only thing we can do. Paul couldn't leave the prison, once he started to praise the Lord. When his chains dropped off and the doors flew open, he stayed. It would have appeared that God had given him a way out but he stayed because he knew that God had something even better for him right where he was.
P

Don't give thanks for the bad thing, give thanks that God has it all in control. Give thanks, because God has a better plan for you. Give thanks, because there is hope for tomorrow. Why? *Because He Said So.*

Ephesians 6:13

"Wherefore take unto you the whole armour of God, that ye may be able to withstand in the evil day, and having done all, to stand."

If you wonder what the will of God is for your life, give thanks. If you wonder how to fix a bad marriage, give thanks. If you need a better job, give thanks. If you need direction and don't know what to do, give thanks. Don't give thanks for the bad thing, give thanks that God has it all in control. Give thanks, because God has a better plan for you. Give thanks, because there is hope for tomorrow. Why? *Because He Said So*.

Prayer

Lord Jesus, I get confused and frustrated when my life doesn't go the way I expect it to. Help me to realize that even though your plans may not be my plans, that I can trust you. I know your word says that all things work together for my good as long as I put my trust in you. So today I choose to trust you,

Because You Said So!

Chapter 6
Value

I was looking through my jewelry box one day. While lifting up some little boxes, I came upon two lariat type necklaces. One was silver with clear glass gems and the other identical except for pink gems. Just looking at those two necklaces brought back memories. They had been a gift from my son when he was about 5 years old. I will never forget his words as I unwrapped the gift he had so carefully purchased for me. Under all of the bright colored tissue, I found the two necklaces, each with more than half of the gems missing.

Christopher's eyes were bright with excitement as he said, "Mama, I found these two necklaces and they were so beautiful. Look, Mama, look, look..they have real diamonds. I know they are real because someone already stole half of the diamonds. I thought they were so beautiful that I bought you two!"

In my heart I chuckled at his little boy happiness and how sweet it was that he thought he had bought me real diamonds. They have always been two of my most precious possessions, not because they have real diamonds (of course they are only glass), but because my little boy said they were real.

My daughter, Marie-Louise did a similar thing when she was about seven. Across the street from our house there was a yard sale. I didn't know that my daughter and one of her little friends had gone to the sale in search of some treasure. Coming back from their shopping adventure Marie-Louise said, "Mom, I got you this." In her hand was a chipped piece of decorative glass missing an obvious top piece. "Mom, look how beautiful this crystal is, I just knew you would love it. Happy Birthday!"

Of course I wore my necklaces a few times, and for a while, that piece of broken glass sat on a shelf in my kitchen window. I have saved them both. Not because they have any monetary value, but because they are among my most precious possessions. Both having much more value to me than they would have to anyone else in the world.

Many people never realize the joy that is theirs just because they are accepted and valued by God.

Thinking about those little gifts, I'm reminded of the gift of Salvation that Jesus gave to us. Being the most valuable and costly gift ever, He sold everything to give this gift to us. And what did we give Him in return? We gave Him ourselves, broken, chipped, worn out, and missing pieces. Gladly He took our gift, and wore us like a precious gem around His neck. He took upon himself our brokenness, our failures, our hurts and pain. Never once has He said our gift isn't good enough. Never once has He rejected our gift.

Looking at our lives, He sees the missing diamonds, and broken crystal, and says, "Look, the Devil has stolen some of your diamonds. Your crystal is cracked and broken. Come, let me replace your diamonds and mend your cracks." Fixing us up, He then declares that we are His most treasured possession.

Malachi 3:17

"They shall be mine, says the LORD of hosts, in the day when I make up my treasured possession, and I will spare them as a man spares his son who serves him.." ESV

I can just imagine what it is like, as He polishes us up and shows us to His Father. "Look Father, look. See what I have brought you. See how beautiful these are? I found this one and she was missing diamonds. You see, the devil had stolen them. I took her and replaced the stolen gems. See how beautiful she is? And this one, see what a beautiful piece of crystal he is? Isn't he just amazing? When I got him he was cracked and broken but I have mended him. Just look at the way the light makes him sparkle." Then, because Jesus said we were of great value, the Father accepts us and puts us in a place of prominence, seated with Him.

Many people never realize the joy that is theirs just because they are accepted and valued by God. Thinking that they have nothing to give, they don't know how easily their broken lives can be fixed. They don't know the pleasure that comes to the Lord when we come to him, no matter the shape we are in. Some think they have nothing to give, or that their gift is too small or insignificant. But that just isn't true.

Have you ever watched a mother or father as they care for their new baby? Carefully they cuddle him, cooing sweet words. Then when the baby makes a terrible stinking mess in his diaper, they will ever so gently lay the child down on a soft little blanket or pad and start to clean the mess away. Never once do they scold the baby for making the mess. They don't get impatient because he made the same mess the day before. They don't yell and scream that it smells bad. No they take their time to clean the child with no regard to whether the mess gets on them or not. There is nothing that baby can do that will make his mommy and daddy displeased with him. He is valued above everything else. You may say, "That isn't much of a gift!" Well, after all, what else does a baby have to offer?

Zephaniah 3:17

"The LORD thy God in the midst of thee is mighty; he will save, he will rejoice over thee with joy; he will rest in his love, he will joy over thee with singing."

In the same way, God cares for us. He loves our gifts. They may not be the best. They may not have any earthly value at all. However, no matter the size or value; with God it truly is the THOUGHT that counts. God isn't worried when we have nothing but filthy lives to give Him. He is just pleased that we came. Touching us, caring for us, like a new born baby, our Loving Heavenly Father washes us clean with the blood of His own Son and makes our gift more than acceptable. Never once is He repelled by the mess of our lives nor does He care that our stink touches Him.

Isaiah 64:6

"But we are all as an unclean *thing*, and all our righteousnesses *are* as filthy rags...."

I have treasured my gifts from my children because they came from their hands. The missing parts and broken pieces only made them more dear and special. I am so happy that Christopher gave me those necklaces and I love the broken vase from Marie-Louise. They have value. Why? Because they said so. They are gifts that were given with love. In the same way God loves you and treasures everything you give Him. There is no gift too small. Every gift given to the Father is cherished and loved. We honor God when we give Him our all even if our all isn't so good. Why? Because God said so!

The Apostle Paul reminds us in **Ephesians** that we have been seated in heavenly places. We have been given a place of honor. I have gone to a few concerts where I had the privilege to sit in the very front. I have been to others where I have had to sit far in the back. Believe me, it is so much nicer to sit in the front. We have been given a heavenly place of honor. We get to sit right up front. God is not ashamed of us. He has not sent us to the back to hide but He has seated us with Him. We were dead in our sin but we have made a life exchange with Jesus. Now we have the honor to sit right up front with Him.

Deep in my heart I heard Him say, "It is the same for me. I look for broken and rejected people. I look for those who will be the perfect canvas of my love, grace and mercy. I find great value in brokenness. Only in the truly broken do I find beauty." How is this possible? *Because God Said So*, of

Ephesians 2:4-10

But God, who is rich in mercy, for his great love wherewith he loved us, Even when we were dead in sins, hath quickened us together with Christ, (by grace ye are saved;) And hath raised us up together, **and made us sit together in heavenly places in Christ Jesus**: That in the ages to come he might shew the exceeding riches of his grace in his kindness toward us through Christ Jesus. For by grace are ye saved through faith; and that not of yourselves: it is the gift of God: Not of works, lest any man should boast. For we are his workmanship, created in Christ Jesus unto good works, which God hath before ordained that we should walk in them.

My friend, we have all come to Jesus, broken and with missing pieces. But He doesn't care. Coming to Him broken and lost, only makes us more dear to Him. He doesn't see what is missing, He just finds pleasure in who we are in Him. He treasures us and likes to show us off to His Father. Did you catch that? He treasures us. He treasures YOU! So when the devil tries to remind you of your worthlessness remember who you belong to. Just remember where you are seated. Remember what Jesus says about you. With excitement in His voice and a twinkle in His eyes, He comes to the Father and says, "Look what I brought to you Father."

Psalms 51:17

"The sacrifices of God are a broken spirit: a broken and a contrite heart, O God, thou wilt not despise."

One day, while on a mission trip, I was searching the beach for shells. I make a lot of jewelry and I had noticed that many pieces of shells and other ocean debris would make beautiful jewelry. Some of my friends started scouring the beach with me. Soon everyone was coming to me with perfectly shaped shells. I knew as soon as I saw them that they would not make the most beautiful jewelry. I looked from their hands full of shells and at what I had collected. My pieces which had been rejected by my friends, were broken and oddly shaped. I knew exactly what made the difference. Only the broken ones would make beautiful jewelry.

It was in that moment that God began to speak to me. Deep in my heart I heard Him say, "It is the same for me. I look for broken and rejected people. I look for those who will be the perfect canvas of my love, grace and mercy. I find great value in brokenness. Only in the truly broken do I find beauty." How is this possible? *Because God Said So*, of course!

Ephesians 2:4-6
"But God, being rich in mercy, because of his great love with which he loved us, even though we were dead in transgressions, made us alive together with Christ - by grace you are saved! -and he raised us up with him and seated us with him in the heavenly realms in Christ Jesus," ESV

Ephesians 2:8
"For by grace are ye saved through faith; and that not of yourselves: it is the gift of God:"

Prayer
Lord Jesus, I give you my life. I give you everything, the good and the bad. Sometimes I feel so broken that I wonder how you can see any good in me. I am so glad that you cherish me and you have brought me on this amazing journey of your love. Even though I don't understand how you could love me, I will believe you,
Because You Said So!

Chapter 7
Stepping Out in Faith

My friend Judy and I took a long trip to the city of Man, in the eastern part of the Ivory Coast. Pastor Edmond organized the trip for us and even traveled with us to make sure everything went well. The reason we went was because Judy had heard the Lord speak to her heart that this particular area needed prayer. So we planned this trip to be a prayer journey. There was one other plan for the trip and that was to find a "young man, with a baseball cap on his head, sitting behind a mask." Judy had seen this man in a vision. She was insistent that we look for him while we prayer walked, because God had told her to do so.

We arrived in Man after a whole day's journey by bus. We got a hotel where Judy and I shared a room and Edmond had another. The next day, we had hoped to hire a taxi to take us all over the city. however, when we started looking for taxis, none could be found. We discovered that the taxi drivers were all on strike and we would have to walk wherever we went. And so we walked. We walked all over the place; walking North and South, East and West. We walked and walked all day in 90 degree+ temperatures. Everywhere we went we prayed that God would be established in this area. We also spent the day looking for the young man sitting behind the mask. As the day grew to a close, I have to admit that I was getting a little weary looking for this young man. We looked up and down alleys and behind every corner. Suddenly, Judy saw the mask she had seen in her vision and guess who was sitting behind it? A young man wearing a baseball cap.

We walked down the driveway where the young man sat. Neither Judy or I could communicate to the man so Pastor Edmond translated for us. Would the young guy be willing to go to a restaurant and have a cold

Coke with us we asked? Suspicion and confusion was all over the man's face. Why would perfect strangers ask to have a Coke with him? Edmond did his best to assure him that we meant no harm and that all we wanted to do was have a talk with him. After some coaxing from Edmond he finally agreed to go to a restaurant with us.

Sitting across the table from our curious guest, Judy began to ask him if he knew who Jesus was. Yes, he knew about Jesus but he was not a Christian. Judy and Edmond were both quite direct with their questions and asked him if he would like to receive Jesus as his Lord and Savior. "No," he responded. "Why not?" Edmond asked. The young man was afraid of persecution. It seemed that our new acquaintance had a lot of friends who would tease him and persecute him if he became a Christian. We then asked if he would be willing to become Edmond's friend, exchange phone numbers and continue talking about Jesus. He did agree to that. Then Judy began to tell our new friend what God had told her about him.

Judy said, "You have been worried because of your mom. You need money to pay some of her medical bills. God sent me all the way across the ocean to find you and give you some money for your mom's medical expenses." Then Judy did something that I don't think that young man will ever forget; I know I didn't. She opened up her purse and took out, what to him was, more than a month's wages. Judy gave him the money, with no strings attached, just *Because God Said So*. Now we had an open door to speak to the young man because God had spoken to Judy and she had followed His voice.

I can still see the look of shock and amazement on that young man's face as Judy asked him if his mom had been sick. Yes was the reply....his mom had been very sick and was still in the hospital as a matter of fact. He did need money to pay her medical expenses. Judy had given him just what he needed. He asked her why she was giving him, a stranger, money. "Because God said so," was her reply.

When I think back about the trip that Judy, Edmond, and I made, I can't help but reflect on the fact that just a few months later, that country was wracked by a civil war that would span over a decade. Today the city of Man has been decimated as hundreds died and thousands fled. I am so glad we didn't wait for another time to go, or question God. We may have never gotten another chance. We went...*Because God Said So*.

In **Acts 9**, the story of Paul's walk with Jesus begins. He had been a strong opponent against the early Christians. Pursuing them and putting many to death, his name was feared throughout the church. One day as he was traveling, Jesus appeared to him in a bright light. He asked Paul, why he was persecuting Him. Paul responded by asking, "Who are you Lord?" "I am Jesus, the one you are persecuting," came the reply. Jesus told Paul to stand up and to go into the city and there he would receive directions as to what to do. When Paul stood, he was blind and needed help to enter the city of Damascus. For three days he could not see. During this time, he had a vision of a man by the name of Ananias who would come, lay hands upon him, and heal his blindness.

At the same time Ananias had a vision from God. God told him to go where Paul was waiting and lay hands on him. God wanted to use Ananias to bring sight to Paul. However, Ananias wasn't so sure he wanted to do that. He reminded the Lord about all of the things that Paul had done. He recounted all of the atrocities Paul had committed and quite honestly, he was afraid to approach Paul. He probably thought that it was a great risk to go to someone like Paul who had the authority to imprison him or even worse put him to death. But the Lord told Ana to go because He had a plan for Paul. Paul would take the Gospel to the Gentiles, Kings, and to the people of Israel. So Ananias went. Why? *Because God Said So!*

> When we take the time to learn to hear His voice, He begins to trust us and tell us things that other people wouldn't accept. There are times that He wants to see how much we trust Him and He expects that we will step out in faith.

Acts 9:15

"But the Lord said to him, "Go, for he is a chosen instrument of mine to carry my name before the Gentiles and kings and the children of Israel." ESV

As Ananias approached Paul he said, "Brother, the Lord Jesus, who appeared to you on the road, has sent me to pray for you." Immediately Paul could see.

We don't know very much about this man Ananias. There are other people in the Bible by that name, but this particular Ananias is almost unknown to us. The one thing we do know, is that he could hear the voice of God and was willing to be obedient to His voice. Obviously, he had counted the cost as he thought about going to see Paul and even questioned God. He knew his life was in the Lord's hands and he was willing to trust God's voice. However, he wanted to be sure. Paul was known to kill Christians and without the protection of God, Paul could have Ananias tortured or worse. This didn't change the Lord's response? Go! That was all Ananias needed to hear. Go! He went, stepping out in faith knowing that God would protect him. The only reason he went to see Paul, was because God told him to.

> Walking with God, trusting His voice, and stepping out in faith, doesn't come easily nor is it cheap. There is a price to be paid. That price can be many things. The first is time spent alone with God. There is no short cut to knowing God's voice. It demands time. Once you have spent time and learned God's voice, you can step out in faith knowing that God is directing you.

Sometimes our walk with God is like that. When we take the time to learn to hear His voice, He begins to trust us and tell us things that other people wouldn't accept. There are times that He wants to see how much we trust Him and He expects that we will step out in faith. I will never forget the days before Fred and I went to Russia. We prayed together and took many long walks wondering if we had really heard from God. Once we were sure, we just took that giant leap of faith and started making plans to go. There was no doubt in my mind. God had spoken and if He said to go, I would go, just *Because He Said So*. I could have never anticipated the troubles we would have after we arrived. But even so, it wouldn't have mattered. We went...*Because God Said So*.

Walking with God, trusting His voice, and stepping out in faith, doesn't come easily nor is it cheap. There is a price to be paid. That price can be many things. The first is time spent alone with God. There is no short cut to knowing God's voice. It demands time. Once you have spent time and learned God's voice, you can step out in faith knowing that God is directing you. There may be other costs involved in your step of faith. For Judy, there was a financial demand as it cost her money for an airplane flight, and other expenses involved in her trip to Man. For Ananias, he had to die to himself, knowing that he might give his life, just to reach out to Paul, a man known for murdering Christians.

Isaiah 50:4-5

"The Lord GOD has given me the tongue of those who are taught, that I may know how to sustain with a word him who is weary. Morning by morning he awakens; he awakens my ear to hear as those who are taught. The Lord GOD has opened my ear, and I was not rebellious; I turned not backward." ESV

Our life with God is a journey, a step of faith. Those who turn back have nothing to offer the Kingdom of God. Many people never realize the plan of God because they are unwilling to spend the time or pay the price. How often have we missed the plan of God because we preferred to sit on the couch, watch TV, or sleep a little longer?

Everyday we have to be willing to say to the Lord, "Here I am. What would you have me do today?" Then, regardless of the cost or the sacrifice, do what He said...*Because God Said So.*

Luke 9:62.

"And Jesus said unto him, No man, having put his hand to the plough, and looking back, is fit for the kingdom of God. "

Prayer
Lord Jesus, I'm going to take a step of faith today. I don't want to miss what you have in store for my life. So today I'm going to spend some extra time with you. I want to hear your voice. I want to be led by you. Here I am, Lord. Speak to me, I want to hear you. Give me ears to hear. I know that I can hear you,
Because You Said So!

Chapter 8
Authority

In **Acts 11**, the apostle Peter had a vision from God, where a sheet was lowered and inside of the sheet were all kinds of unclean animals. As Peter looked at the sheet, the Lord began to speak to him saying, "Take and Eat." Peter was shocked and told God, "Not so. I have never eaten anything unclean before." God responded by telling Peter that he should not call anything unclean that God had declared to be clean. This vision came to Peter three times.

Peter realized that in this vision, God was speaking to him about the "Good News" of Jesus' death and resurrection, being available for salvation to the Gentiles. God was telling Peter to go and preach the "Good News" to people that Peter would have rejected. Now he was compelled to go to the Gentiles...*Because God Said So*. People criticized Peter and argued that he should not take the message of Jesus to anyone who was not circumcised. Not only that, but they insisted that Peter shouldn't even eat with them. However Peter would not be moved by their arguments. He knew he was doing what God wanted him to do. He knew he was supposed to accept the Gentiles. He knew that he had the authority to open the way for people who were uncircumcised. Why? *Because God Said So*.

When I was sixteen, I wanted to get my drivers license. As soon as I could, I got a learner's permit and my dad started to take me out driving. I am not the speediest driver. I don't like to drive fast and I never did. I would drive slower and slower until my dad would tell me to operate the steering wheel and he would push the gas pedal. Even today, if I am driving, my husband will comment "You know, we have to get there today!"

In my high school we had a driver's education class. As soon as I could enroll in the class, I did. I had a little experience, but I really didn't know how to drive. When I did drive, I drove so slow that my dad was just working on speeding me up. We hadn't yet gotten to the part where I would have to parallel park the car. I didn't even know what a K turn was.

On my first day of class, the instructor made an offer to the students. He was taking a group of students, who had been in the class for a while, to take both their written and driving exam. He had one seat left in the car and he offered that spot to anyone who would like to go. No one seemed to be jumping at the chance, so I raised my hand and said I wanted to go. Later that night, I told my dad about this opportunity and asked him if it was OK with him that I go. He said yes, but later told me that he only said yes, because he thought that I would fail and it would be a learning experience for me. He thought it would help me to be better prepared when I was truly ready to get my license.

As followers of Jesu
as members of His fa
we have also been giv
authority. We can de
our own snakes and
scorpions whether rea
figurative. We defeat
accusing words of fea
using the name of Jes
Panic attacks, though
suicide, and
worthlessness, are all
overcome by the auth
we have in Jesus' nam

The next day, our car was full of expectant new drivers, each hoping to come home with the prized permit to drive. I took the written exam and passed with no problem. I had to wait my turn to take the driving test, which was driving a Pennsylvania State Trooper around town. When it was my turn, I jumped into the driver's seat, buckled myself up, checked my mirrors, and turned the car on. The trooper said to pull out of the parking lot and when I got to the street he said I should turn right. I started to exit the parking lot and suddenly, he got all red in the face and was very angry. I knew I hadn't done anything wrong. I hadn't done anything really, but he sure was mad. Turning away from me he started shouting to no one in particular. "I gave that guy a ticket yesterday for parking in that spot. Can you believe he has the nerve to double park in the same spot today?" He was looking at a delivery truck that was double-parked, blocking the road. Turning to me he said, "Turn back into the parking lot and drive back up to the door." When I got back to the door we had just left from, he said, "Get out...you passed!" I don't think I even turned the car off. I just parked and got out.

Imagine my surprise when he said I had passed. My father's surprise was even greater when I came home waving my coveted driver's license. Then to my surprise, when I asked if I could take the car out for a drive, he said yes! My sister and I drove to town, about 4 miles away and the first thing I did was bump the parking meter...I didn't know how to drive. But I had a license. Why? Because a Pennsylvania State Trooper said so.

The authority I have to drive and operate a car dates back to that one day; when a distracted State Trooper declared that I had passed the driving exam and that I was indeed a competent driver. No one ever questions my license as I show it for an ID. No one ever questions if I can drive. My license looks like everyone else's and carries the same authority as any other driver's license. Not only that, but I now have a New York State driver's license and I have had an international license because at one time, I had a valid Pennsylvania license. From that day until now I have the right to drive because a Pennsylvania State Trooper said I could.

Peter had great authority. When he was accused of wasting the gift of salvation on the Gentiles, those who the Jews thought were not good enough, he explained about his vision and the great sheet being let down from heaven. He told how the voice of God had told him to take and eat and how he had at first refused. Then Peter finished his story with God telling him that he should not call unclean what God had called clean. From that moment on there was no more argument against Peter. They accepted what he had to say because Peter said that God had spoken to him through this vision.

There may be times in your life when you wonder if you have authority. In **Luke 10:19,** Jesus told his disciples that He had given them all authority to tread upon snakes and scorpions. It is reasonable to conclude that as His modern-day disciples, we also have that same authority. Jesus came to earth, filled with all authority, given to Him by His Father in Heaven. As followers of Jesus and as members of His family, we have also been given authority. We can defeat our own snakes and scorpions whether real or figurative. We defeat accusing words of fear using the name of Jesus. Panic attacks, thoughts of suicide, and worthlessness, are all overcome by the authority we have in Jesus' name.

John 14:12-14

"I tell you the solemn truth, the person who believes in me will perform the miraculous deeds that I am doing, and will perform greater deeds than these, because I am going to the Father. And I will do whatever you ask in my name, so that the Father may be glorified in the Son." NET

Why did Jesus say that we have all authority in His name? Because He died and offered us the opportunity to have a life exchange with Him. He would live in us, and we would live in Him. Because He lives in us, we now have the authority to use His name. He, said so. I don't understand the power of Jesus name. Many theologians have tried to explain all of the whys and hows but everyone has to come back to this....we have authority...*Just Because God Said So.*

Traveling around in different countries comes with many experiences both good and bad. To do what we have done in West Africa, we have had to cross over many borders, sometimes as many as three in one day. The lines of cars are sometimes very long and there are many people trying to pass to the next country as well. The heat can be stifling. My husband has a gift that most people don't have. He seems to know how to cross borders, that are littered with red tape, easier than anyone I know. His secret? He approaches all of the border guards, government officials and security personnel as if he has the ultimate authority. He has even been known to say to someone who is giving him a hard time, "Do you know who I am?" Now of course, he is no one of importance in those countries, but in the Kingdom of God he has great authority. It is with this authority that he gets us over those borders time and time again.

Luke 10:19

"Look, I have given you authority to tread on snakes and scorpions and on the full force of the enemy, and nothing will hurt you." NET

One year on my annual trip to the Philippines, I took several ladies with me. One day I told everyone that we had a big trip ahead of us.

We would be traveling to a village that required that we cross fifteen rivers. I gave this little thought as I had traveled this road many times before. I had a book to read and was calmly reading as we made the trip.

After we had been traveling for about two hours, friend Judith commented that she would like to know what the title of my book was. She assumed that it had to be some kind of amazing book as I seemed to be captivated by it, disregarding the road we were traveling on. I told her it wasn't anything special and that it wasn't even that interesting. I only wanted to finish it so I could start another. She told me she had assumed the book was amazing since I didn't seem to notice the road. I asked her what was wrong with the road and she began to express her concern. About that time we started a steep decent into

> Because He died and offered us the opportunity to have a life exchange with Him. He would live in us, and we would live in Him. Because He lives in us, we now have the authority to use His name.

a raging river bed. She said, "See that? We are driving right into the river." I reminded her that I had said we would cross fifteen rivers. Her response, "Yes but I assumed there would be bridges!"

I had forgotten about the missing bridges. I have little fear as I travel and missing bridges seemed to be only a minor technicality. I have learned to walk in the authority God has given me. I don't have time to be afraid and if I do get afraid, I do my best to remind myself of the authority I have as a child of God.
O
We have been given great authority. We have the power to defeat the works of darkness in this world. We don't have to be afraid of tomorrow. I know that my life is in the hands of the Lord and that I have authority wherever I go. Why should I fear? After all...I go, *Because God Said So*!

Matthew 8:8-9

"The centurion answered and said, Lord, I am not worthy that thou shouldest come under my roof: but speak the word only, and my servant shall be healed.

But the centurion replied, "Lord, I am not worthy to have you come under my roof. Instead, just say the word and my servant will be healed.

For I am a man under authority, having soldiers under me: and I say to this man, Go, and he goeth; and to another, Come, and he cometh; and to my servant, Do this, and he doeth it."

Mark 6:7

"Jesus called the twelve and began to send them out two by two. He gave them authority over the unclean spirits."

Prayer
Lord Jesus, now I understand that I have authority. I can live my life in faith knowing that you walk with me and that I don't have to be afraid of tomorrow. I have spent so much time worrying that I'm not sure how to walk in faith trusting in you. But today, I will try to hold your hand and trust in you,
Because You Said So!

Chapter 9
The Impossible

One day as Jesus was passing by a group of fisherman, He looked at Peter and said, "Follow me." He didn't have a meeting where all of the fishermen were invited. He didn't interview potential disciples, ask for references, or require a background check. No, He just looked at Peter and said, "Follow me." Jesus then added, "I will make you a fisher of men." I have often wondered what was in Jesus' eyes or the look that he gave, that convinced Peter to follow. This fisherman had lived his whole life by the sea and fishing defined who he was and yet, in one simple moment, everything changed and he was no longer employed as a fish catcher. He would learn the ways of men. He would be taught by the master. He would be transformed day by day as he followed Jesus. Someday he would even become a great apostle, teaching others about the Son of God. But on this day, he only had one thing to do. He had to let go of his past, embrace Jesus, and follow him. Why would he do this? Because Jesus said so.

It wasn't impossible for Peter to change. He changed, one step at a time. Peter was compelled to follow Jesus and everyday he was transformed. The same is true for us. Jesus calls us and miraculously, God begins the work of transformation. Day by day, step by step, we become a new person.

There will always be times in our life when we don't know why we feel compelled to do what we do. The whys don't even matter so much as the obedience. One day, in Africa, an old woman approached me. She held out her hand and it was obvious she was asking for money. I didn't give it much thought as I took out some coins and placed them in her hand. I didn't even look at what I was giving her. I just reached in my purse and took the first ones that came to my fingers and gave them to her. As she took them we both looked, and the coins I had given her were worth much more than most people give her. She smiled a thank you and I thought, why did I do that? Because somewhere in my heart, Jesus said so.

It's possible to do the will of God without much thought. The voice of God often comes to a committed soul, when his spirit embraces the thoughts of God. As you strive to do His will and as you commit everyday to Him, it becomes easier and easier to do what He wants. Soon it becomes second nature to do what He is saying. The next thing you know, you will be doing something without thinking and realize it wasn't you doing the act but it was Jesus within you. You responded to the compelling voice of God and it became an act of obedience birthed from past obedience. Wouldn't it be easier to live our lives if we could always live this way! Walking and doing the will of God, just because He said so, even if you did not actively seek out the voice of God.

> It's possible to do the will of God without much thought. The voice of God often comes to a committed soul, when his spirit embraces the thoughts of God.

A few years ago, while I was in West Africa, I received an email from my cousin Becky. She and her husband, Doug, had been working towards adopting twins from Asia. They had received word that public relations with that country and the USA had been strained and as a result, adoptions would be closed. All adoptions needed to be finished before a certain date. Becky and Doug knew that their adoption plans were not that far along and that it would be impossible to complete the process in time. Fortunately most of the monies they had spent were towards the American side of the adoption proceedings and they only lost about two hundred dollars of what had been invested, however, they had to switch countries. In the email Becky sent, she asked if we, Fred and myself, had any twin girls in our orphanage. Well the orphanage wasn't ours exactly, however we had a very close relationship with an orphanage in Benin. (It did eventually become part of our ministry). Amazingly, we did have twin girls. Not only were they twin girls but they were very close to the age Becky wanted, and adoptable, something that is not always true.

We started the proceedings and by many miracles of God, we were led to believe that this adoption could not only be done, but that it would be easy. Well, it wasn't exactly easy; however, God had a plan and soon photos were sent to the girls of their new family and Fred and I took photos of the girls to send to Becky and Doug. Plans were made, papers were signed, and the only thing that was needed for the plans to finish, was for Becky to appear before the Judge and sign the final papers. We were told that the Judge would let us know when this could be done in enough time, so that Becky could travel to Africa. I had returned to America for a couple of months and I told Becky that when the call came I would travel with her back to Africa to get the girls.

We got the call and three other friends agreed to travel with us. Off we went, expecting to sign papers, and bring those girls home. The first thing we did was have a meeting with the Family Court Judge. As we sat in her office, she began to ask one question after another. There seemed to be a few questions that she was most concerned with. "Why do you want to adopt these two girls? I see that you have two other children. Why would you want more children when you already have two?" Becky's answer was quick and spoken with great conviction...Because God Said So!

What we didn't know was that employees of the courts had gone on strike. No papers could be typed up and it was a nightmare. Every day Becky struggled. She had been given the girls as soon as we arrived in Africa and she was bonding to them even with the language barrier. Many days went by and they became weeks, as we waited for the strike to come to an end. Becky began to miss her family in NY. They were missing her too. Questions that we hadn't even thought about began to become a reality. What should we do? How could Becky justify leaving her family for so long and yet how could she abandon the children that were just beginning to realize that she was their mother?

Every day we would pray. Prayer groups all across the USA were praying. We would get encouraging words like, "Don't give up. It will all work out." Yet day after day Becky's heart was breaking as she was trying to reconcile her need to be home with her family and her need to be there for her new daughters. The only thing that kept Becky in Africa was the fact that God had told her to adopt twin girls. Armed with that fact, securely established in her heart, she stayed and pressed on, even though hot tears threatened to spill at any moment.

Then the day came when we realized the strike was going to go on for several more months and we were faced with airplane tickets that couldn't be changed again, as we had changed them several times already. In one day we realized we would have to leave Africa without the girls. That was one of the hardest days any of us had ever faced. How could we leave those little girls after we had promised them a new life?

What we didn't know at the time, was that God had already been preparing the twins. Before we knew that we had to leave, one of the girls had begun telling our friend Pastor Augustine that she was going to go home with him. She was jumping and smiling as she told him that little bit of information. Little did we know, at the time, that the two girls would indeed go home with Augustine and his wife Rebecca.

I will never forget that evening as our day was about to close and we had to tell the now four-year olds that we were leaving for America, that very night, without them. We finished the arrangements for Pastor Augustine and his wife to keep the girls until the paperwork could be straightened out. Then we went to a restaurant and tried to keep the evening light and happy. We didn't want the girls to be sad and afraid.

Eventually the time came when we had to tell the girls what was about to happen. I had told Augustine that he would have to explain the situation to the girls as we didn't even speak their language. He called them over and started talking to them. What he said was nothing short of prophetic and full of faith.

"Mommy has to go to America tonight and get things ready for you. She wants to know what you want in your new home?" They thought for a while and even conferred with each other. "Well," they said, "Could we have a broom? We could help mommy clean if we had a new broom." On and on they asked for simple things: a shirt, bread and cheese, even electricity. Smiling through tears Becky was shaking her head yes. She would make sure they had everything they listed and wanted. They believed the words, Augustine spoke. They were not afraid. They had the faith of a little child and believed, just because he said so. By the end of our little conversation, the two girls jumped up and down in excitement, that mommy was leaving and getting their house ready. As a matter of fact, in their excitement they started running outside, not even saying goodbye. They wanted mommy to go, so that when it was time, she would return and come get them. She would...because she said so.

In what must have seemed like a lifetime to Becky and her family in New York, was in reality only four short months when my husband flew from Africa to New York with Becky's two little girls. Two precious children, who were so excited to see their new American family, flew off luggage carts as they spied Becky and ran to her and the rest of their new family. The impossible happened. Why? *Because God Said So.*

Psalms 68:6

"God setteth the solitary in families: he bringeth out those which are bound with chains: but the rebellious dwell in a dry land."

When Becky and her husband Doug started their adoption journey, it seemed like an impossible plan. They didn't have any money. They were living in a small apartment and Doug was going to school. With two children at home, their finances were strained to the max. However, God had spoken and so they pursued two little girls, just Because God Said So. Many things happened that tried to discourage them. First, their original idea of adopting from Asia fell through. Then even after we found two little girls in West Africa, Becky had to commit to a journey to Africa; a trip she didn't really want to

> Jesus promised that we would have life, and that life, would be filled with abundance. I don't believe that the abundance Jesus speaks of is just enough to get by. No! Abundance by its own definition, is more than enough.

take. Becky had never spent time away from her family and she had no desire to fly to Africa. Then as our two week trip evolved into a two month trip, with expenses piling up and missing her family, Becky was faced with having to leave the two little girls in Africa and coming home with nothing but the promise from God. She did all of this only...*Because God Said So.*

Four months after the girls had arrived in the USA, I was traveling in the same area in Benin when a missionary friend came to visit me. She had heard that I was trying to help my cousin adopt some African children. She was concerned because she had lived in Benin for twenty-six years and, in all of those years, she had never seen a successful adoption from Benin to the United States. She had tried, without success, to help several people adopt children from Benin to the USA. Her years of work had only brought sorrow to both the children and their hopeful adoptive parents. I just sat and listened to all of her sad stories. She finished with, "I just wanted to warn you before you and your cousin spend a lot of money. Adoptions to the US don't work here." She finished with, "You will never get those little girls to America. It's impossible."

I listened to all she had to say and when she finished I smiled and said, "Thank you, but they are already in America. The papers are finished, the adoption is legal and they have been living with my cousin and her family for four months now."

Little did I know that what she said was true. It was impossible to adopt children from Benin to America. We had done the impossible...*Because God Said So!*

> No longer are we a people who have no hope, but we are citizens of heaven. We now have the promise of a better life with Him. Why do we believe this? Because He said so, that's why!

I Corinthians 10:13

"There hath no temptation taken you but such as is common to man: but God is faithful, who will not suffer you to be tempted above that ye are able; but will with the temptation also make a way to escape, that ye may be able to bear it."

Jesus said He would never leave us or forsake us. He promised that before troubles even come, that he would have already been there providing a way out of those troubles. He said that He was going to prepare a place for us, so that at the end of our life, we would have a place to live with him for all of eternity. No longer are we a people who have no hope, but we are citizens of heaven. We now have the promise of a better life with Him. Why do we believe this? Because He said so, that's why!

John 14:1-3

"Let not your heart be troubled: ye believe in God, believe also in me. In my Father's house are many mansions: if it were not so, I would have told you. I go to prepare a place for you. And if I go and prepare a place for you, I will come again, and receive you unto myself; that where I am, there ye may be also."

Just like two little excited girls, we can go on day after day, knowing that God is concerned with our heart's desires. There is nothing we can imagine that will surprise Him. He is busy preparing just what we want. Not only that, He is happy and excited to do it. I will never forget the look on Becky's face as she shook her head, smiling through shining tears saying, "Yes, I will make sure that there is electricity in every room of your new home." To those who have grown up in America, the promise of electricity in every room and having bread and cheese doesn't seem so exciting, after all, those things are just understood. But for two little girls who had grown up in an orphanage, with little or no electricity, sleeping on the floor, and eating watery porridge everyday, their request was beyond their wildest dreams.

John 10:10

"I am come that they might have life, and that they might have it more abundantly."

Jesus promised that we would have life, and that life, would be filled with abundance. I don't believe that the abundance Jesus speaks of is just enough to get by. No! Abundance by its own definition, is more than enough. We serve the God of more than enough. God is so much more than we can imagine or ever need that one of His names is El Shaddai. And El Shaddai actually means "more than enough." It means, the God who provides in abundance, the God of more than enough.

When I think about those two little girls, leaving the orphanage and moving into Becky and Doug's home, I can't help but compare the two places. Those little girls asked for bread, cheese and electricity but what they got were beds and blankets, shoes, toys, new clothes, winter boots and coats. They left Africa as orphans and arrived in New York with a new mother, father, sister, brother, grandmas, grandpas, and an unlimited amount of aunts, uncles, and friends. What they asked for was small compared to what they got. They got a new life that was abundantly more than they could ask or even think. Our limited knowledge of what is available for us, often limits what we ask of God. It was like that for the twins. They really didn't know what to ask for. Similarly we don't really know what to ask of God because we don't know what is already available for us.

Ephesians 3:20

"Now unto him that is able to do exceeding abundantly above all that we ask or think, according to the power that worketh in us,"

When you give yourself to God, like Peter responded to Jesus, or like the twins gave themselves to Becky, your life takes on new meaning. Impossible situations become possible...All *Because God Said So*!

Prayer
Lord Jesus, help me believe that you can do anything. You can fix my life, my marriage, my kids, and my finances. If you tell me to believe for the impossible, I will believe because nothing is impossible with you. I believe, Because You Said So!

Chapter 10
Faith

Romans 10:17

"So faith comes from hearing, and hearing through the word of Christ" ESV.

Romans 12:3

"For I say, through the grace given unto me, to every man that is among you, not to think of himself more highly than he ought to think; but to think soberly, according as God hath dealt to every man the measure of faith."

Why do we have faith? The answer is so simple. We have faith...*Because God Said So.* The Bible tells us that we have all been given a measure, or portion of faith. It also says that faith comes by hearing the word of God. What is the word of God? It is the written "Word," known as the Bible. It is God's spoken word, made real in our hearts or our minds, or even sometimes an audible voice spoken by Him or someone He is using. I have heard the voice of God many times in my heart. Sometimes as I read my Bible, I hear God speak. I have had ideas pop into my mind that I know come from the mouth of God. I have had people tell me something and instantly I have known it was God speaking. However two times He spoke to me in an audible voice.

Now I know that may be hard for some to believe but if you know me at all you would know that only the actual voice of God would have convinced me to do what he was asking me to do. I have never liked babysitting. I did some babysitting when I was a teenager but I could probably count on one or two fingers the times that happened. My husband, who loves kids, would have gladly entertained the idea of a children's ministry. He has always picked up everybody's baby and cooed and smiled at them. Me? Well most people have never even seen me hold a baby. Don't misunderstand. I love my son and he is and will always be the exception; however other people's babies were just that! Another person's baby. So as we began our work in ministry, I made it very clear that I would not teach children's Sunday School classes. The few times I did teach, the experience left me ragged and stressed-out for days. When we became missionaries in the Ivory Coast, I told the pastor we were working with, that I would gladly do whatever he needed or wanted me to do but under no circumstance was he to expect that I would ever, work with children.

> Why do we have faith? The answer is so simple. We have faith, *Because God Said So.*

One day in our Bible school some of our students said they had seen a vision and had a word from God for me. The word however, wasn't one I was ready to hear. They said, that God was going to give me another child. They saw me with a baby. Now, of course, I didn't believe them. How could God give me a child? I could no longer have a baby because of the cancer I had had. I wasn't looking for a baby to adopt, that was the furthest from my mind. Obviously God had not spoken to them.

One morning, our pastor/friend in Africa, came to our house looking very sad. One of the widows in the church had died in the night. She had been a prayer warrior in the church, had spent much of her time praying and was loved by everyone. I didn't know this widow but while the pastor spoke, something began to churn in my spirit. The phrase, "Did she have children?" kept coming to my mind. I asked the pastor about her children and he said that yes she did. He thought she had five or six children. Immediately I felt that I should do something for these orphans.

I couldn't get the impression to go away and I began to ask around about the orphans. No one seemed to know anything. No one could answer my questions. How many children are there? What are their ages? Are they boys or girls? Are they sick or well? I couldn't get any information.

I had to return to the United States for some dental work and while I was there I would email Fred and ask him to let me know what he had found out about the kids. However he found out nothing. Day after day I would write and I got no information. I figured I could buy the children things while I was in the States. I needed information as I didn't know their ages, sizes, or even their gender. I didn't know what to do. Frustrated every night, I would pray and ask God to speak to Fred and make him answer my questions. Then I would complain to God that He had told me to do something for these children and Fred wasn't doing it. After all, he was the one who liked kids. Surely, doing something for these kids was his responsibility. I didn't know that back home in Africa, Fred was trying to find out the answers to all of my questions but the children had been moved and no one seemed to know how to answer him. I complained to the Lord that Fred wasn't giving me the information I needed in order to do something for these children. My frustration only increased day by day. I needed God to tell me what I should do.

One night about 2 AM, while I was sound asleep, a hand touched my shoulder and gave me a shake to wake me up. I opened my eyes and no one was in the room. Then I heard a voice. Yes you heard me right. I heard a voice that was not in my head or in my imagination. I heard a real voice. I knew it was the voice of God. "The smallest one is your daughter," the voice said. Well, I didn't know what to think about that, so I didn't tell anyone what I had heard. The next night was a repetition of the night before. I checked my email, complained to God that Fred had not sent me the information I wanted, and then went to sleep. At about 2 AM, once again, a hand shook my shoulder and woke me up. As I opened my eyes and looked around the room, I saw no one but I heard the voice again. "The smallest one is your daughter."

"OK," I said, "You don't have to tell me three times." I knew God had spoken but I still didn't know how to process that information. I had learned, that in Africa, there are many ways to be a mother or father to a child. Children will often call someone who pays their school fees, their mother or father. The same is true of anyone who sponsors a child in any other way such as paying medical expenses, rent or food.

A spiritual mentor, out of respect, is often called mom or dad. So what exactly did God mean when He said the smallest one was my daughter?

When I returned to Africa, I told Fred what had happened and what God had said. We went to see our friends, the pastor and his wife. As we began to tell them of our desire to help the children of the dead widow, especially the smallest (we found out the smallest was indeed a girl), the pastor's wife began to cry. She told us how all of the other children had homes to go to but there was no place for the smallest one. Then she said, "This child would be so easy to adopt. She has all of her papers." I looked at my husband and he looked at me. "How easy?" I asked. Within days, she was ours.

The smallest one was indeed my daughter. All those prophetic words that I had received at the Bible school about having another child had come true. Not everyone has to have God speak in an audible voice, however that is exactly what I needed the night God spoke, giving me the child prophesied months before.

I will never forget Fred's words as he told me that I had to be the one who wrote home and tell everyone that we were adopting a little girl. He said that if he wrote, no one would believe that God had spoken to me. They would all think that Fred had pressured me to adopt the little girl.

Now years later I am very happy that I listened to the voice of God. With that voice came an assurance that God was interested in this little girl and because of that, I have great expectations for her. I have also discovered what I would have missed in never having had a daughter. I am very thankful for her and so glad that I said yes to God's voice. However, having said all of that, those first days were hard. You see, I adopted her *Because God Said So*. I didn't have compassion on her. I had no pity for her situation. I had never met her, how could I? I didn't know anything about her. I didn't gaze into her cute little eyes and suddenly fall in love with her. No! I took her ....*Because God Said So.*

So often we expect that just because God directed us to do something, that from that day on, there would be no problems. That just isn't so. Sometimes we have to work out the plan of God, as we live our lives. Faith is not seeing everything perfect and in order, but it is believing in something that cannot be seen. God said that a little African girl, was my child. We had to work through red tape and fill out forms for her immigration to the United States. From the very beginning we had to work out the plan. We had faith that someday, she would not only be ours legally but that she would be ours in our hearts, and that she would become a citizen of the United Sates of America. Her life changed, and with her, so did ours.

Matthew 9:29

"According to your faith, be it unto you."

One day while traveling in the south of Palawan, an island in the Philippines, some friends and I came to a small church where we had two days of meetings. We were encouraging the local pastors and their congregations which is often what I do when I am on a mission trip. On the last night, I shared on the necessity of forgiveness. I explained how, people often withhold forgiveness, thinking they are punishing the one who wronged them, when in fact they are punishing themselves. I ended my message with an altar call where many people came forward for prayer.

So often we expect that just because God directed us to do something, that from that day on, there would be no problems. That just isn't so. Sometimes we have to work out the plan of God, as we live our lives. Faith is not seeing everything perfect and in order, but it is believing in something that cannot be seen

After my friends and I prayed for everyone, I noticed that many seemed to linger near the front of the church. Some were singing while others continued to pray. My niece Angelina was on this trip and when I looked for her in the room, I saw that she had a young girl in her arms. The girl was crying and Angelina just held her. I wasn't sure what the girl was crying about but I knew it was a good thing Angie was there. She just prayed and prayed holding onto the sobbing girl.

The next day, as we were leaving, the girl handed Angelina a note that explained her tears. About three or four months past, she had run away from home and had found herself working for a family in Manila. She wasn't interested in being a Christian anymore. She wanted to see the world and make money. Her whole family prayed for her and was looking for the day when she would come back home.

One night while the girl was sleeping in the home of her employer, the eldest son of the house, high on drugs, came into her room and stabbed her twenty-six times. I know this was true because I saw the scars. The girl was taken to the hospital and her prognosis was grim. Eventually she recovered enough to travel home to be cared for by her family. Realizing her folly, the girl gave her heart to Jesus and dedicated her life to serve him. It just so happened that the village we were in, was her home town and she had come to the meetings with her family. As a matter of fact, her sister had been traveling with us.

Hearing about forgiveness she decided to forgive her attacker, and as Angelina held her, she cried out tears of forgiveness, directed at the man who had stabbed her. The next day she wrote us a lovely letter telling us her whole story. She said she didn't want the man to hurt her anymore, by keeping unforgiveness towards him, in her heart. She wanted to forgive him and get on with her life. How could she forgive that man? She was just a young woman and yet, as soon as she heard God speak to her heart she forgave, unconditionally. In her note she said that she had never felt so free. Why did she forgive? *Because God Said So*.

Mark 11:24

"Therefore I say unto you, What things soever ye desire, when ye pray, believe that ye receive them, and ye shall have them."

Most people don't realize that it is a step of faith to forgive someone. It is faith that says, "It matters not if the one who wounded me deserves forgiveness, I choose to forgive!" Why do we forgive? *Because God Said So*. We forgive in faith, believing that God is able to keep us and heal our heart. Only forgiveness opens a heart and brings relief to a wounded and fragile soul. We don't forgive for the other person. No! We forgive for ourself.

Many people refuse to forgive because they believe that the person who hurt them doesn't deserve to be forgiven. Holding a grudge, they withhold forgiveness, believing they are punishing the offender. Unforgiveness becomes their weapon of punishment. Unfortunately it is not the offender who is being punished. It is the one withholding forgiveness who suffers from a self-inflicted punishment.

Deuteronomy 32:35

"To me belongeth vengeance, and recompence; their foot shall slide in due time: for the day of their calamity is at hand, and the things that shall come upon them make haste."

One day I had a conversation with my daughter, Marie-Louise. She had been hurt by another young woman and was very angry. "I hate her!" She repeated over and over. I told her she shouldn't say that and that she should forgive. Her response was, "Mom! She doesn't deserve to be forgiven!" I told her that forgiveness was not for the offender.

No! Forgiveness is for the wounded. We forgive for ourselves. It doesn't matter if the person deserves it or not. We forgive to release the peace of God in our own spirit. I wanted to help her understand, what I was trying to say. Finally she ended our conversation with, " It's easy for you to forgive. I am not you!" Praying that God would give me another opportunity to help my daughter understand the power of forgiveness, I let the matter drop.

> Most people don't realize that it is a step of faith to forgive someone. It is faith that says, "It matters not if the one who wounded me deserves forgiveness, I choose to forgive!"

A few days later I found myself complaining to God about Marie-Louise's dog. For some reason her dog had started chewing my stuff. She chewed my sock and my shoes. She ate my chewing gum and even my cough drops. She went in search of my things, going so far as to stick her nose into my coat pockets looking for treats. I was so angry at that dog. One day I had had enough. I started to complain about "that stupid dog" who only ate my things. I just couldn't understand why it was, that the dog never ate Fred's or Marie-Louise's things.

In the middle of one of my rantings, God spoke to me. "Forgive the dog." Forgive the dog? I couldn't believe that God had said such a thing.

I said, "But God, it's a dog. I don't have to forgive a dog. Why would you even say that?"

As soon as those words came out of my mouth, God spoke again, "I didn't ask you to forgive the dog for the sake of the dog. No! You forgive for your sake. If you don't forgive the dog, you will allow murmuring and complaining to have a home in your heart. Forgive the dog!"

I got the message loud and clear. Quickly I ran to my daughter's room and told her I had forgiven her dog. She gave me a funny look and said, "Mom, it's a dog. You don't have to forgive a dog!"

"Ah but I do," I said. "I will forgive the dog for my sake and not the dog's."

I wanted to withhold forgiveness because I was sure that dog would chew my things again and I had more faith in the dog misbehaving than I did in her leaving my things alone! It takes faith to forgive. Forgiveness demands that we forget the past and look forward to a new future, not for the offender but for ourselves, knowing that our life is in the Lord's hands and that we can trust Him. I forgave the dog...*Because God Said So*!

Prayer
Lord Jesus, I have been so hurt. My heart is weary and I am afraid to forgive. I don't want unforgiveness to ruin my life but I am afraid. Help me to put my trust in you. I can have faith that if I forgive, you will make things right for me,
Because You Said So!

Chapter 11
The Ability To Fight

In the book of **Judges chapters 6-8** we see the story of Gideon. The Angel of the Lord appeared to Gideon and greeted him saying, "The Lord is with you courageous warrior." Gideon's reply? "If the Lord is with us then why are we so oppressed? The Lord has abandoned us." The angel of the Lord replied to Gideon that he (Gideon) had the strength to lead God's people out of their slavery. Gideon then becomes the super hero of this story. He was an unlikely poor man who, according to him, was the least of the least. There was no one as low as he was, yet he gathered an army and defeated the Midianites. How did this nobody, the least of the least, achieve such great victory? Because God Said So, and Gideon believed it.

John 10:10

"I am come that they might have life, and that they might have it more abundantly."

Jesus said that he came to give us life, and that more abundantly. Think about this. Jesus spoke and something was established or created. Jesus spoke, and abundant life became available to you and me. However, many of us look at the abundant life that Jesus promised and like Gideon, our response is, "If Jesus promised us abundant life, then why don't I have it? Where are all of the promises that God has promised me? Why am I still having trouble? Why does it seem like I can never get ahead in life?" The response from the Lord is the same as for Gideon. "Go in the strength you have... Am I not sending you?" (NIV)

> You too can have victory in your life. You may be afraid but courage is not courage until it is found standing in the face of fear.

Perhaps you feel like there are many great faith believing people who are stronger and more experienced in spiritual battles than you are. You may think that there is nothing in you, that is strong enough to fight. You have been beaten down and feel like you have no courage at all, as a matter of fact you are down right afraid. Gideon felt that way too. In the same way that the angel of the Lord spoke to Gideon, God is speaking to you. "Go in the strength that you have." You too can have victory in your life. You may be afraid but courage is not courage until it is found standing in the face of fear. It took no courage for King David to fight the Philistines, he was a trained warrior and knew how to fight. Gideon on the other hand, had no training and no past experience to draw from. He was afraid. It took great courage for him to gather an army and go into battle against their oppressors, the Midianites.

Later in **Judges 7:10**, the Lord said to Gideon, "If you are still afraid, go down to the enemy's camp and listen to what they are saying about you." So what did Gideon do? Because he was afraid, he went sneaking into the enemies' camp late at night, and heard how God had made the Midianites afraid of him. Can you imagine the surprise on Gideon's face as he heard from his enemies' own lips, how mighty and powerful he was? He took that information back to his camp and, shoring up his courage, he gathered his army and went to war.

What is so amazing about this story is that Gideon didn't have to fight. All he had to do was stand, believing that God would help him. God caused a great confusion and the Mideonites fought themselves. Gideon didn't have to do anything but proclaim the victory and show up to the battle. Gideon defeated the Midionites. Why? Because God said he would!

Ephesians 6:13

"Wherefore take unto you the whole armour of God, that ye may be able to withstand in the evil day, and **having done all, to stand.**"

I can remember times when my mom and dad would tell me to do something and my first response would be, "Why?" My parents would then say, "Because I said so." I think most children have had someone say those words to them at least once in their life. I know I did on many occasions. Is there any phrase more frustrating? No explanation, no other instruction except, "Because I said so." Years ago when I was just a small girl, I was in the car with my mom. I must have felt like a pretty big girl because I was allowed to sit in the front seat of the car. It was dark out and it had been raining. As we came to a stop at an intersection, a grungy looking man came up to the car. My mom, said, "Debby, lock the door." I quickly hit the lock button just seconds before the man tried to open the car door. My mom has often reflected on that story by saying, "I don't know what would have happened if Debby hadn't locked the door as soon as I spoke." I had well learned to obey just because my mom said so.

One of the hardest things to learn is to trust in the words, "Because I said so." It is hard because it takes faith to trust in the person saying those words. However in Psalm 29, David expressed his awe at the power of God's voice. It thunders. It is full of majesty and shakes the forests. God has unlimited power in His voice. Over and over in the Psalms David writes to express to the reader, of the awesomeness of God's voice and the power His voice has when He fights for us.

Gideon had to trust in the words of God. Gideon had to step out in faith and go to the battle, just Because God Said So. Jesus said you will have life abundantly and it requires faith to believe in those words. We don't know how it happens, just that it does. It takes faith to believe that we have eternal life. How does that work? Theologians from ages past have tried to understand eternal life and it all comes down to faith. "Because God said so." We have abundant life, provision, hope, peace, the list is endless. We are healed because of the wounds that Jesus suffered for us. How could his wounds give us healing? Exactly how do all these things happen? *Because God Said So!*

Psalm 29:3-9

The voice of the LORD *is* upon the waters: the God of glory thundereth: the LORD *is* upon many waters.The voice of the LORD *is* powerful; the voice of the LORD *is* full of majesty.

The voice of the LORD breaketh the cedars; yea, the LORD breaketh the cedars of Lebanon. He maketh them also to skip like a calf; Lebanon and Sirion like a young unicorn. The voice of the LORD divideth the flames of fire. The voice of the LORD shaketh the wilderness; the LORD shaketh the wilderness of Kadesh. The voice of the LORD maketh the hinds to calve, and discovereth the forests: and in his temple doth every one speak of *his* glory.

When we adopted our daughter Marie-Louise, she was a citizen of the Ivory Coast, West Africa. As time went by we filled out papers for her to immigrate to the United States. One day she received an envelope addressed to her from the President of the United States of America. Inside was a letter that said, "Congratulations! You are now a citizen of the United States of America." That letter was signed by no other than the President of the United States of America, George Bush. That night at church she proudly showed her letter to everyone declaring, "I bet you don't have a letter from President George Bush."

Months later, while living in the Ivory Coast, the country suffered a coup d'état. This once peaceful country erupted into a long drawn out civil war. The US Embassy called and emailed; informing us that if the situation in the country worsened, they would come and help us. They would bring us food or water or even help us get out of the country, if it became necessary. They wanted to know how many Americans were living in our house. We said three, Fred, myself and Marie-Louise. Marie-Louise, who had been born in that country would now be protected by America's finest. American Marines would lay down their lives for her. Why? Because President George Bush said she was a United States Citizen. She had to do nothing. She didn't have to fight in the war. She didn't even have to be afraid because the battle surrounding her was being fought by someone else.

John 14:27

"Peace I leave with you, my peace I give unto you: not as the world giveth, give I unto you. Let not your heart be troubled, neither let it be afraid."

Just like Gideon, you may still be afraid. You may have even had the same kind of conversation, with God, that Gideon had. Maybe you have complained that if God was with you than why are there so many problems in your life? Why is there trouble and financial problems? Why do I feel so far from God? The answer is the same as it was for Gideon. Have faith in God. He has made promises that he will fulfill. You can believe, just *Because God Said So*.

All around us there are battles being fought. Some are spiritual, some emotional and some physical but in the middle of the battle, the words of Jesus ring out, "I have given you life and that more abundantly.".

The Bible tells us that greater is He that is within me than he that is in the world. That verse is powerful. That means that even if you don't think you have power, you do. Not only that but your enemy is afraid of you. He knows Jesus lives in you and he trembles. If you could sneak into the enemies camp, right now, you would hear him telling how afraid he is of you and how afraid he is that you might start believing the truth of the power that is inside of you.

I John 4:4

"Ye are of God, little children, and have overcome them: because greater is he that is in you, than he that is in the world."

We have been adopted into the family of God and because of that, we are now citizens of heaven. All around us there are battles being fought. Some are spiritual, some emotional and some physical but in the middle of the battle, the words of Jesus ring out, "I have given you life and that more abundantly." As a citizen of Heaven we are now guaranteed abundant life. Even when all is in turmoil, we still have abundant life. Not just life someday in heaven but abundant life here and now, in the midst of your storm. Heaven's finest, Jesus, has laid down His life for anyone who calls on His name and has made a life exchange with Him. Jesus lives in us, we live in Him, and He fights our battles for us. How does this happen? *Because God Said So.*

Prayer

Lord Jesus, sometimes I feel like Gideon. I am nobody and there is no strength in me. I know that you said that I have strength so I believe you. Help me when I forget that you are great inside of me and that you are fighting my battles. All I have to do is trust in you and remember that no matter what storm I am in, I can rest knowing you are there with me,

Because You Said So!

Chapter 12
Out Of Our Comfort Zone

Almost every great man or woman in the Bible had a season in their life where God required them to step out of their comfort zone. They found that the calling of God became activated when they stepped away from what was familiar. In faith, God expected them to walk into the unknown. Moses, Gideon, Esther, Ruth, Peter, Samuel and David, to name a few, had to come to a place, in their relationship with God, that took them away from their natural gifting and talents. They had to leave their families behind. They had to embrace something that was unknown to them. God required them to step out of their comfort zone into the calling God had for their lives.

I Kings 19:19

"So he departed thence, and found Elisha the son of Shaphat, who was plowing with twelve yoke of oxen before him, and he with the twelfth: and Elijah passed by him, and cast his mantle upon him."

Among all the many stories in the Bible, where God changed a persons' life just by the power of His word, one stands out to me. That would be the story of Elisha. Elisha could not have anticipated, that one day the prophet Elijah would be walking down the road near to where he was plowing. Nor could he have imagined, that the prophet would make his way to Elisha and throw his cloak over him, symbolizing that he should follow Elijah as a man of God. At that moment everything in his life changed. He was no longer a farmer but now he was in the school of prophetic ministry. Why did this happen? God had spoken to Elijah and told him to anoint Elisha, the son of Shaphat from Abel Meholah, to take his place as prophet. Elijah anointed Elisha, because...God had told him to.

From farmer to prophet must have been a giant leap. However Elisha jumped in with both feet and pursued his new occupation with great fervor. Not only did he excel in following his mentor Elijah but he endeavored to become even greater, wishing for a double portion of the anointing that was on Elijah. Following the direction of the Lord, Elijah took Elisha on as an apprentice. God was about to take Elijah away and God wanted a prophet to remain among His people to speak for Him. Imagine what it must have been like for Elisha. I don't think, that even in his wildest dreams, he ever thought, that he would one day be a prophet. He was working hard, doing whatever the Lord had put in his hand to do. He was a successful farmer, however God had another plan. Elisha took his plow and cattle, burnt them as an offering to the Lord and followed Elijah. He was literally "burning his bridges" and his old life, behind him.

Almost every great man or woman in the Bible had a season in their life where God required them to step out of their comfort zone. They found that the calling of God became activated when they stepped away from what was familiar.

My dad once told me about the frustration he had, as a dairy farmer. He was tied down to a job that he did very well, yet one that he despised. Every day he would rise before sunset to milk the cows and work until late at night, feeling like he was trapped. Seldom did he have a day off and even those days required that he milk the cows before he left the farm and again after the sun went down. He never dreamed that someday the Lord would take him out of that job and send him to Bible school. He could have never imagined that his obedience would one day take him around the world, visiting places he had only dreamed of.

My dad had given his life to the Lord and was trying to understand what God wanted him to do. For several nights in a row, he had a reoccurring dream. In this dream he saw a sign on the side of the road. That sign said, "Visit Elim Bible Institute." He knew exactly where to find this school because it was in the same general area where he would go to buy and sell cows. So, believing that God was speaking to him, he drove to the school enquiring about classes. The next Monday, he was a full time student. He never wanted to go back to school. He had hated school as a boy but he stepped out of his comfort zone, and went back to school because God had told him to.

After three years of school he pioneered a small church in Pennsylvania, then pastored a church in the Washington DC area. Finally he moved back to Western New York and pioneered another church. This is where his life took on a whole new dimension.

He had always been a wonderful preacher. He never thought he could preach but God had spoken to him about story telling and how he could use his stories to preach just like Jesus did when He told the parables. Everyone loved his messages that his stories inspired. I can still remember some of his sermons, almost word for word. But he was also gifted as a teacher. He read the Bible through more than three hundred times and his insight was inspired by the Holy Spirit. A Bible school in the area asked him to come teach and from there, people from around the world would ask him to come to their country and share the Word of the Lord.

One day he told me, as we sat under a palm tree on the island of Palawan, "Debby, I thought I would live my whole life on that farm, trapped. Today, I feel like I'm living in a dream." He loved the people of the Philippines and especially those on the island of Palawan. He would often state that someday he would love to live out his days on that island. "You'll find me under one of these Palm trees," he would often say. How did he get there? He got there because years before God spoke to him in a dream. He went to Bible school because God said so.

I like to think of my dad as a man who followed the word of the Lord, much like Abraham in Genesis 12. Abraham left his country and in doing so, he left his comfort zone just to follow the word of the Lord.

Genesis 12:1

"Now the LORD had said unto Abram, Get thee out of thy country, and from thy kindred, and from thy father's house, unto a land that I will shew thee."

I have discovered that often the gifting or talent God has given us is not always directly related to our calling. Where as Elisha and my dad were all successful in their hard working endeavors, those endeavors were not the final say in their destiny. They were prepared to become a prophet or pastor by being faithful to whatever God had put in their hand to do.

My son Chris, was very gifted in the area of computers. When he was just a young man of sixteen, he was building custom made computers. It was obvious he had a gift. He could do things that no one else could do. He studied how to read and write computer programs. People trusted him with their money and credit cards to build computers and then he would network those computers together. His dream was to become the best he could be. Obviously God had given him talents. And he could have made a good living working on computers but that was never the plan of God for his life. Today he is an attorney, with a desire to become involved in politics. Why did he become a lawyer? Because God told him to. Why does he want to be in politics? Because God told him to. Were his computer talents bad? No! His gifting helped to pay the way for his calling but they were not the end product.

When I was a teenager, I assumed, that because I could sing I would become a famous singer one day. I dreamed of records (now I'm showing my age) and concerts. I could see myself traveling all around the United States singing. I assumed that because I had a gift, that this was the call of God on my life. For years I chased after that dream, being disappointed when nothing happened. I even made a sample recording that I sent to over fifty companies. Almost all were returned unopened, with a note telling me that without an agent, they wouldn't even listen to me. It never occurred to me that perhaps that was not in the plan of God. Why would God give me the gift and that gift not be the plan?

Years later, after my failed demo recording, God began to take me all over the world in mission work. Once when I was discouraged while living in Africa, I emailed my friend Judy. I asked her to pray for me. I felt like I was stuck in figurative mud. I knew God had something better for me but I felt like my life was going nowhere fast. She wrote back to me and said, "It's time to start writing the books."

Well I have to confess that I laughed. I told my husband that I didn't have any idea what to write or how to even start. Books? You have to be kidding! The more I thought about it the more I came under conviction that I should listen to my friend. The Lord told me that I had asked Judy to pray. I also knew that God spoke to her when she prayed for people and that I should trust that she had heard from God this time too. So, I sat down to write, and in three or four days I had written my first book, Suddenly. Why did I write? Because God Said So.

Our gifting or talent can sometimes become the enemy of our calling. Without a clear word from God, we go from ability to ability wondering why we don't feel satisfied with our day to day life. We wrongly assume that because we have a gift that we know where and how God wants to use it.

> When God has another plan, we need to be willing...to walk away from what is familiar, step out of our comfort zone and follow him. We do this regardless of the cost, many times not even knowing why. We will do these things... Because God Said So!

Our gifting or talent is our familiar comfort zone. We do that job well. I am very comfortable singing in front of thousands of people. I can even sing in French, a language that I am, in no way fluent. Singing is easy for me, I am almost never, even a little bit, nervous as I sing. But that has not been my calling. I had to step out of my comfort zone and depend on the Lord to help me, as I write and speak about what God has said to me.

I have never been a very good speller. As a matter of fact, I can remember telling teachers who would criticize me about my poor spelling, that I would never, ever, need to know how to spell. I was sure that no matter what God had for me, that spelling would not be important. After all, why would a singer need to know how to spell? No one could have guessed that one day we could all be great spellers with the help of a wonderful little computer program called "Spell Check". Spelling is not my gift. However , putting those words together has become my calling. Why did I start writing books? Because God Said So.

Because of my mission work and because of my books, I have the opportunity to sing to thousands of people. This gift is a blessing that God uses in my life but it is not my calling. My son used his gifting to help pay his way through school, anticipating his future as a politician. Had Chris assumed that he should spend his life working on computers, just because of his gifts and talents, he would have missed the call of God on his life. Had I given up pursuing God because my musical aspirations didn't come true, I would have missed some of the greatest experiences of my life. Is it wrong to be a singer, a farmer, or computer tech? No, but if God has another plan we need to be willing, like Abraham, Elisha, or my dad to walk away from what is familiar, step out of our comfort zone and follow him. We do this regardless of the cost, many times not even knowing why. We will do these things...Because God Said So!

Prayer
Lord Jesus, I don't like stepping out of my comfort zone. I feel comfortable in surroundings that I am familiar with. But I know that if I want to grow in you, I have to be willing to take a step of faith. Lord I know that you only have my best interest in mind and that you have a plan for my life. So if I need to take a step of faith and trust you, I will. I can trust you,
Because You Said So!

Chapter 13
Transformed

I was about seventeen when my sister Cheri and I went to a neighboring town to do some shopping. On our way home, I saw something in the road. As we got closer and closer, I saw that there was a giant raccoon in front of us, laying on the side of the road.

When I was a small girl my dad loved to go, coon hunting. He would tell us glorious stories of romping in the swamps with his favorite coon hounds. Spending most of the night he would tromp from place to place in search of the biggest most awesome raccoon he could find. This was something he did for both fun and to make money. He would catch a coon and skin it, selling the pelt for a few extra dollars. When I saw that huge raccoon laying on the road I realized it was not just any ordinary coon before me. No! This one was exceptional! It was huge. I didn't think I had ever seen a coon so big.

All I could think about was how much money my dad could get from such a prize. I pulled the car over, opened the trunk of my dad's new car, and Cheri and I bent over that mound of coon flesh. It took the two of us to heft the thing into the trunk, that's how big it was. All the way home I was so excited to show my dad what we had gotten for him. My enthusiasm was soon dashed as I could see that my dad wasn't very excited with my find. How was I to know that, that coon which I had seen in the road was in fact a very large bloated, dead, road killed raccoon full of bugs and rotting skin.

I think what I remember the most is that my dad didn't yell at my sister and me. He just thanked us and dealt with his smelly, maggot filled gift. What I had thought would be a great gift was in fact a mound of stinking rot. Not only did it smell bad but that stink was now all over my dad's new car. Now, my dad had to get the coon out of the trunk before it made an even bigger and stinkier mess.

> Somehow God takes the gifts we give and makes them into good things. In the garden of God's love He redeems our mess.

Sometimes we come to God bringing him gifts. What we don't know is that our gifts are like that raccoon. We think that what we offer is special and good, when in fact, they are nothing. Like that rotting coon, they get their stink all over everything. Our gifts are worthless. They come with new problems like, how to get rid of the mess without getting the stink on you?

Anyone who has had the joy of bringing a new baby home, can tell you that they come with messes. When a baby soils his diaper the cleanup usually means the stink is everywhere. This doesn't worry the new mom or dad. No! They are happy that their baby makes the mess. If their child didn't, something would be wrong. The mess is anticipated. When we mess up, God doesn't care. The stink doesn't matter to him. Our mess is also expected. God is not offended by the way we come to him. Jesus took our stink and put it on himself. The only time we offend the Spirt of Grace is when we refuse his free gift, trampling underfoot the blood of His sacrifice.

Hebrews 10:29

"How much worse punishment, do you think, will be deserved by the one who has trampled underfoot the Son of God, and has profaned the blood of the covenant by which he was sanctified, and has outraged the Spirit of grace?" ESV

We used to have a rabbit and he used to make enormous messes that could be smelled throughout the house. He was supposed to be housebroken but sometimes I thought it was our house that was broken, not him. He would run around Marie Louise's room, chewing up cables and cords and leaving a mess in his path. However Marie Louise didn't care, because she loved him.

Like our rabbit, there will always be messes in our lives that God has to clean up. We do damage to relationships, our health, our finances, you name it. We destroy many things but the grace of God is always available for us because He loves us. We are forgiven. Somehow God takes the gifts we give and makes them into good things. In the garden of God's love He redeems our mess.

2 Corinthians 3:18

"And we all, with unveiled face, beholding the glory of the Lord, are being transformed into the same image from one degree of glory to another. For this comes from the Lord who is the Spirit." ESV

2 Corinthians 5:17

"Therefore, if anyone is in Christ, he is a new creation; the old has gone, the new has come!" NIV

Jacob was a man in the Bible who was transformed. In the book of **Genesis**, his story begins by him grabbing his twin brother's heel as they are being born. He wanted to be the first one born. However, Esau his brother was the first to be born and from that time on, Jacob chased after everything that belonged to Esau. Through trickery and with the help of his mother, he deceived his father into giving him Esau's rightful firstborn blessing. Because of Esau's anger over being tricked, Jacob fled and went to live with his uncle Laban. This time Jacob met his match. Laban was twice the deceiver than Jacob had ever been.

Jacob fell deeply in love with his uncle's second born daughter, Rachel. Laban made an agreement with Jacob that if he worked for seven years, he could have Rachel as his wife. The seven years felt like only one day because he loved Rachel so much. Finally the wedding day arrived. The bride, covered with a veil, declared her covenant vows with Jacob her bridegroom. He in turn made his covenant pledge.

Jacob took his new bride to his tent, only to find out in the morning, that he had not married Rachel but her homely sister Leah. To say Jacob was angry would be an understatement. He quickly ran to his new father-in-law and complained. I can just imagine his shouts of fury as he accused Laban of deceit. One could even say, that at that moment, Jacob reaped what he had sown. He had deceived his father and now he was face to face with one who was twice the conniver than he was. Now he would have to work another seven years for Laban in order to marry the woman he loved.

In **Geneses 29-32** the story unfolds as Jacob is deceived over and over again. His wages were changed and he was cheated until he couldn't take any more. So gathering his wives, his children and his flocks he ran away from his father-in-law. One night, weary from traveling, fearful of an encounter with his brother Esau, he wrestled throughout the night with a stranger. He didn't know that the man he was fighting with was God himself. As the morning sun began to come up, the man told Jacob to stop fighting and to let him go. Jacob responded, telling the man that he wouldn't stop until the man blessed him. It was then that the man began to tell Jacob that his name was now changed.

Genesis 32:26-28

"And he said, Let me go, for the day breaketh. And he said, I will not let thee go, except thou bless me. And he said unto him, What is thy name? And he said, Jacob. And he said, Thy name shall be called no more Jacob, but Israel: for as a prince hast thou power with God and with men, and hast prevailed."

Somehow in the midst of all of Jacob's troubles, God had been transforming him. The name of Jacob means, "one who grabs or one who wrongly takes the place of another." He had taken what belonged to his brother Esau, and then found himself dealing with a man who was worse than he was. God used Laban, his Father-in-Law, to change Jacob. Jacob the cheater was little by little becoming Israel. No longer would he be Jacob the one who cheated but one who is now upright, a Prince with God, one who had fought with both men and God, and who had won, all Because God Said So!

There is an interesting character in the Bible that we know of as Mark. He was a cousin to Barnabas and had traveled with Paul and Barnabas. Unfortunately he had deserted his cousin and Paul, leaving them in Pamphylia. This was so upsetting to Paul that he refused to allow Mark to travel with him and Barnabas on their next trip. Paul and his good friend had a great argument over this, so much so that they parted ways. Paul then took Silas on his journey instead of Barnabas. Obviously Mark's desertion was upsetting to Paul. We don't know exactly what happened but it was serious enough that Paul refused to travel with him.

One would begin to wonder if there was any restoration for a man so rejected by the great Apostle Paul and yet Mark found his way into the elite group of men favored by Paul. Obviously he was restored and later in some of Paul's writings he makes mention of Mark as profitable to his ministry and a fellow laborer. The young man who had been rejected was transformed.

2 Timothy 4:11

"Only Luke is with me. Take Mark, and bring him with thee: for he is profitable to me for the ministry."

Philemon 1:23-24

"There salute thee Epaphras, my fellowprisoner in Christ Jesus; Marcus (Mark), Aristarchus, Demas, Lucas, my fellowlabourers."

How this happened we don't know but I think most of the credit has to go to his cousin Barnabas. Barnabas saw something good inside of Mark and thought he should have a second chance. We know that Barnabas was an encourager and he must have invested in Mark, spending time with him everyday as they traveled. Mark was worth it because Barnabas said so.

Romans 12:2

"And be not conformed to this world: but be ye transformed by the renewing of your mind, that ye may prove what is that good, and acceptable, and perfect, will of God."

We have the same opportunity as Mark to be transformed. Daily the Holy Spirit can renew and change us. However many things such as television, internet, or music all compete for our minds. We need to be diligent because God is speaking and we need to be careful that we don't lose the ability to hear him. There is nothing wrong with those things however when they take the place of God's voice, we forget who we are. Not only that but we forget what God's voice sounds like and we soon become the failure the devil wants us to be. How can we be all that God wants us to be if we can't hear him any more?

Psalms 51:10-12

"Create in me a clean heart, O God; and renew a right spirit within

me. Cast me not away from thy presence; and take not thy holy spirit from me. Restore unto me the joy of thy salvation; and uphold me with thy free spirit."

The transforming power of God changes us from glory to glory. No longer are we misfits but we are complete in Him. We never have to struggle to "fit in" any more. We are complete in Christ.

Dale Carnegie once famously said the following: "It isn't what you have, or who you are, or where you are, or what you are doing that makes you happy or unhappy. It is what you think about." You see, we think about what we believe. If our beliefs are flawed then our thinking is flawed. We have to choose to believe what God says about us. Paul encourages us that we can be transformed in our mind. This means our thinking can change. Depression can be broken and thoughts of worthlessness can be erased.

The transforming power of God changes us from glory to glory. No longer are we misfits but we are complete in Him. We never have to struggle to "fit in" any more. We are complete in Christ. Our old life with it's failures and deformities is gone and in it's place is a new creation. We are transformed! Because God Said So!

Prayer
Lord Jesus, change me. Change me to be more like you.
Change me so that I can be all you want me to be.
Transform my mind so my thoughts are like yours and
make me into the person you want me to be. I can be that
person,
Because You Said So!

Chapter 14
God Within

The phrase, "Kingdom Of God" is often shrouded in mystery. This often misunderstood Kingdom, is preached about and sung of, in just about every gathering of Christians. However few have any idea what it is all about. How about you? Have you ever wondered what the Kingdom of God is and how it can be found? The answer is really very simple. The Apostle Paul said that the Kingdom of God is not meat or drink but righteousness, peace, and joy. And Jesus said, the Kingdom of God is within you!

Romans 14:17

"For the kingdom of God is not a matter of eating and drinking, but of righteousness, peace and joy in the Holy Spirit," NKJV

Luke 17:21-22

"And when he was demanded of the Pharisees, when the kingdom of God should come, he answered them and said, The kingdom of God cometh not with observation: Neither shall they say, Lo here! or, lo there! for, behold, **the kingdom of God is within you.**"

Knowing and understanding the Kingdom starts with our life-exchange with Jesus. We call this being Born Again. It is the exchange of our life for that of Jesus' life. The Apostle John said that Jesus is knocking at our heart's door and waiting for us to open the door and let him come in. We make this life-exchange when he comes into our heart and we enter into his. We are no longer our own but we belong to

Jesus and to His eternal Kingdom. His Kingdom, the Kingdom of God, now exists within our own spirit. All we have to do is open our spiritual eyes and believe that it is there. This Kingdom is then manifested as righteousness, peace, and joy.

Jesus reveals His kingdom in our hearts. It can not be found in a distant location, or in selfish desires, but in the hearts and lives of those who respond to Him.

John 3:3

"Jesus answered and said unto him, Verily, verily, I say unto thee, Except a man be born again, he cannot see the kingdom of God."

Revelation 3:20

"Listen! I am standing at the door and knocking! If anyone hears my voice and opens the door I will come into his home and share a meal with him, and he with me." NET

John 10:10b

"I am come that they might have life, and that they might have it more abundantly." NKJV

Serving Jesus, in the Kingdom of God, is the most rewarding and yet challenging thing you will ever do. Rewarding because the benefits are not only for this life but for all of eternity. Challenging because once we come to the cross and accept the free gift of salvation, we then make a life-exchange with Almighty God. Jesus lives in us and we live in Him. We are now citizens of another kingdom. That is, *The Kingdom of Heaven*. This life-exchange then demands that we learn to live in this Kingdom. Anyone who has studied the history of British monarchy will notice that when someone marries into the royal family, the new spouse then has to learn the ways of the Kingdom. They do this by practice and discipline. It isn't easy but they know that if they want to fit into this new lifestyle, then they must change. The Kingdom doesn't change, but they do. Likewise, when we become part of the family of God, we begin a process that makes us suitable for the Kingdom of God. We are changed from glory to glory, step by step.

Jesus reveals His kingdom in our hearts. It can not be found in a distant location, or in selfish desires, but in the hearts and lives of those who respond to Him. This is understood through Jesus' words when He said in **John10:10** that He came to give us life and that more abundantly. This abundant life is characterized by righteousness, peace, and joy. We are righteous through the blood of Jesus. No matter how we come to Jesus, His blood washes us clean and we are no longer condemned by our sin. This amazing righteousness is ours even when we don't deserve it. We have peace in our life-exchange that is beyond all understanding. It is a peace that preserves us when everyone around us is in turmoil. Joy is also ours in this wonderful exchange. It is a joy that can not be explained, it just is. Why is this? *Because God Said So*!

IPeter I:8

"Whom having not seen, ye love; in whom, though now ye see him not, yet believing, ye rejoice with joy unspeakable and full of glory."

Philippines 4:7

"And the peace of God, which passeth all understanding, shall keep your hearts and minds through Christ Jesus."

Philippines 4:19

"But my God shall supply all your need according to his riches in glory by Christ Jesus."

In the Kingdom of God we have abundant life not only in this life but also for the life to come. We have the opportunity to receive from God more than we can possibly ask or even think...every need is supplied. There is no end to the provision of God. When David sinned by taking the wife of Uriah as his own and then having Uriah killed, God said something very interesting. He said, "I gave you (David) all that belonged to your predecessor, King Saul. I gave you everything and if that had not been enough, I would have given you more." Today God is saying those same words to you and me, "If I haven't given you enough, I will give you more." Wow! What an amazing God we have. He is a God who delights in blessing His children. Just like a natural, earthly father would bless his children, our Heavenly Father blesses us.

2 Samuel 12:8

"And I gave thee (David) thy master's house, and thy master's wives into thy bosom, and gave thee the house of Israel and of Judah; and if that had been too little, I would moreover have given unto thee such and such things."

Luke 12:31-32

"But rather seek ye the kingdom of God; and all these things shall be added unto you. Fear not, little flock; for it is your Father's good pleasure to give you the kingdom. "

A good father disciplines his child and my dad was no exception. If I did something wrong when I was small, my daddy would spank me or discipline me according to the wrong I had done. I never wanted to displease my daddy because I loved him and I knew he loved me. When he did discipline me, I never once thought he I didn't love me anymore. I was completely secure in the fact that he loved me and that he would do anything for me. Because of this, I never wanted to disappoint him.

It was at the same moment that David was about to be disciplined by God, that we see the depth of David's heart. David never wanted to disappoint his heavenly Father. It was his greatest fear that because of his sin, he would become like King Saul and lose the presence of God. During this traumatic time in David's life, he wrote **Psalm 51** saying, "Create in me a clean heart oh God. Renew a right spirit within me. Cast me not away from your presence. Don't take your Holy Spirit from me."

One should not confuse discipline and punishment. These words demonstrate two different things. Discipline means to raise, nurture, cultivate, develop, and instruct. Punishment means to cause or inflict pain because of wrong doing.

In every family there are rules and if you break the rules you come under discipline. In the Kingdom of God there are also rules. Unlike the Law of Moses that condemned us, these rules are different. Rules like, whatsoever you sow you will also reap, show us that to live a life of blessing we need to be a blessing. For those who sow in the Kingdom of God, the blessings of the Kingdom are increased. We reap so much more by sowing love to the Lord our God with all of our heart, our soul, our mind and our strength. If we sow disobedience, greed and ingratitude our harvest will be cut short by our failure to live a life of gratitude and we will reap a harvest of sorrow.

Galatians 6:7

"Be not deceived; God is not mocked: for whatsoever a man soweth, that shall he also reap."

Hebrews 12:28

"Wherefore we receiving a kingdom which cannot be moved, let us have grace, whereby we may serve God acceptably with reverence and godly fear:"

Yes it is true, we are blessed regardless of what we do. That blessing is called God's undeserved favor and it showers us with blessings even when we don't deserve them. In addition to that, there is also that amazing Heavenly bank account that is constantly being filled with blessings as we serve the Lord making deposits of love, kindness, faith, hope, encouragement, you name it. If you walk with God you will fill your account and it will provide you with many great assets that can be withdrawn, whenever you need them. The dividends will multiply and there will be no shortage in your life.

Romans 14:17

"For the kingdom of God is not meat and drink; but righteousness, and peace, and joy in the Holy Ghost."

You are in the Kingdom of God and the Kingdom of God is in you. You are no longer of this world. As a matter of fact, you are a citizen of a heavenly kind. Today, movies are made glamorizing aliens, vampires, witches, and wizards. Hundreds of thousands flock to the movie theaters in search of a way to fill the emptiness of their soul. They are hungry for something that answers the questions that nag at their hearts, "What happens when I die? Is this all there is to life? " Their spirits cry out for more, because they were created in the image of God and they are looking for something that is not of this world. People are hungry to understand the spirit world and without Jesus they are left with the spirits of darkness. Because of this, these evil spirits work overtime trying to keep people from knowing the truth of Jesus Christ and His wonderful gift of eternal life. They fight anyone who stands for the truth.

> You have the victory and you no longer belong to yourself, you belong to another. That other is Jesus; and like Gideon, He will fight for you. .

In every kingdom there are times of battle. Because of this, we are obligated to fight. Dear friend, don't be discouraged because of the battle. Remember Gideon? All he had to do was show up for the battle and God fought for him. The enemy of your soul, would like to discourage you, and make you afraid to fight, or even make you give up and walk away; but don't give in. Don't allow Satan to talk to you. He is a liar and the father of lies. He will discourage you if he can.

John 8:44

"Ye are of your father the devil, and the lusts of your father ye will do. He was a murderer from the beginning, and abode not in the truth, because there is no truth in him. When he speaketh a lie, he speaketh of his own: for he is a liar, and the father of it."

You have the victory and you no longer belong to yourself, you belong to another. That other is Jesus; and like Gideon, He will fight for you. A few years ago I was traveling to the Philippines with a team of friends including my father. Our group was completely exhausted when we arrived in South Korea for a layover. We all crashed in a heap on some reclining chairs and slept for what seemed like hours. In the middle of my sleep a stranger came up to me. Thinking I had overstayed my welcome on the chair, he slapped me. He wanted me to wake up and let him have my recliner. I was sleeping with my niece and pretended not to realize what he wanted. He went away and came back, this time slapping me harder. I slid closer to my niece and gave the man my chair. Later when I told the group what had happened, my dad said, "Why didn't you wake me up? I would have fought for you." My father would have gladly fought for me.

Our Heavenly father will also fight for us. All we have to do is show up to the battle and let him fight. In the same way, my husband Fred is obligated to fight for me, should I have the need of a protector. When I married him, I no longer belonged just to myself, but I belonged to him and at that moment he was obligated to fight for me. How much more will Jesus fight for us as we enter the battlefields of our life.

Acts 14:22

"Confirming the souls of the disciples, and exhorting them to continue in the faith, and that we must through much tribulation enter into the kingdom of God."

We have infinitely more power, gifts, talents and authority when we realize that the power of the Kingdom is within us. All of these are already inside of you the minute you made this incredible life-exchange with Jesus. At this point the Kingdom begins to grow in you. Don't misunderstand me. The Kingdom is already within you, perfect and complete. All that is necessary, is for your understanding of the Kingdom to grow, and as it does, more and more of the Kingdom is revealed . The truth is, the Kingdom of God is already within you. It is there, because Jesus said so!

John 8:32

"And ye shall know the truth, and the truth shall make you free."

My friends, as you have come to the end of this book, it is my desire that you would know the truth and as Jesus said, it would set you free. The truth is this, you are loved, you are forgiven, you are special and you can make it. You will be blessed, you will prosper and have more than enough. You can hear God's voice and have direction. You have favor, and hope, and you can do the impossible. You have been transformed, and restored, and can overcome all things . Just *Because God Said So*!

Prayer
Lord Jesus, I am free. I am healed. I am victorious. Everything I am, I am because of you. If you say that I am good, then I am good. If you say I am saved, I am saved. If you say you love me then, you love me. Who am I to doubt your words. Help me to remember that I can trust you, Because You Said So!

.